My Mama, Cass

My Mama, Cass

A Memoir

OWEN ELLIOT-KUGELL

BOOKS

New York

Jacket design by Terri Sirma
Jacket photograph by Henry Diltz/Getty Images
Jacket copyright © 2024 by Hachette Book Group, Inc.

Hachette Books
Hachette Book Group
1290 Avenue of the Americas
New York, NY 10104
HachetteBooks.com
Twitter.com/HachetteBooks
Instagram.com/HachetteBooks

First Edition: May 2024

Published by Hachette Books, an imprint of Hachette Book Group, Inc. The Hachette Books name and logo is a trademark of the Hachette Book Group.

The Hachette Speakers Bureau provides a wide range of authors for speaking events. To find out more, go to hachettespeakersbureau.com or email HachetteSpeakers@hbgusa.com.

Books by Hachette Books may be purchased in bulk for business, educational, or promotional use. For information, please contact your local bookseller or Hachette Book Group Special Markets Department at: special.markets@hbgusa.com.

The publisher is not responsible for websites (or their content) that are not owned by the publisher.

Print book interior design by Amnet Contentsource

Library of Congress Control Number: 2024931060

ISBNs: 9780306830648 (hardcover); 9780306830662 (ebook)

Printed in the United States of America

LSC-C

Printing 1, 2024

For my mother

Ellen Naomi Cohen (Cass Elliot)
September 19, 1941–July 29, 1974

For my best friend

Misty Marie Mehas Romero
September 5, 1967–June 2, 2023

CONTENTS

CONTENTS

AUTHOR'S NOTE

ONE MAY WONDER HOW I AM ABLE TO WRITE ABOUT a period of time that I wasn't alive for, and I can only say this: I have been lucky enough to have been told many stories about my mom by her friends over the years. So many, in fact, that sometimes it's difficult to remember exactly *who* has told me *which* stories, but I have done my very best to recall. Because my mother was a guest on so many TV shows and was interviewed extensively, I have been able not only to watch videos but also to read the many interviews that she gave. I'm so incredibly grateful to have been able to draw on those interviews and videos, as inadvertently it seemed that she'd told part of her story, in her own words, even though she's not here today to do it herself. I've also relied on the memories of some of my mom's musician friends, some told to me in person, and others appearing in their own recalling of their lives in print. The stories in this book have all been included to the best of my recollection, in the spirit of telling a complete story and including multiple points of view.

FOREWORD

M OM DROVE A MIDNIGHT-BLUE CADILLAC CON-
vertible with white leather seats and personalized blue-
and-gold California license plates that read ISIS. Isis, the
Egyptian goddess of life and magic, was undoubtedly someone my mother considered very cool.

I loved riding in that car with her, listening to her sing
along to the radio. Her voice was strong and sweet, easily the
most recognizable of the four-part harmony that had made
the Mamas and the Papas famous. To millions of her fans, she
was known as "Mama" Cass Elliot, the Earth Mother figure of
the Los Angeles hippie scene of the late 1960s. But to me, she
was just my mom.

Sometimes, I would sing along with her from the backseat. One afternoon in 1974 as we headed out to run errands
together, we cruised down Laurel Canyon Boulevard, past the
fabled Country Store in the middle of the canyon, and down
into the heart of Hollywood. We were riding down Fountain

Avenue when "Top of the World" by the Carpenters came on AM station KHJ. As we turned left down La Cienega, she encouraged me to sing along.

I felt shy about singing with her because her voice was so extraordinary. So I sang quietly to myself until I felt more secure, then allowed my voice to get louder as my confidence grew.

I'm on the top of the world
Looking down upon creation
And the only explanation I can find
Is the love that I've found ever since you've been around
Your love's put me on the top of the world

My mom's bracelets jangled on her wrists as she sang and steered the car down Sunset Boulevard. She always wore four gold bangles, three from Tiffany & Co. and one made by Cartier. The bracelets made a clinking sound like soft wind chimes as she used her hands to gesture during conversation, or just when she moved about.

My mother loved the trappings of her success. She would visit Tiffany & Co. on Fifth Avenue whenever she was in New York City and was known to saunter about the store wearing a huge yellow canary diamond that she could never afford to buy but loved to fantasize about.

By 1974, my mother was embarking on a solo career. She had two weeks' worth of sold-out shows booked at the London

Palladium that summer and I was going to spend the time in Baltimore, Maryland, with my Grandma Bess, whom I adored, and who adored me in return. Grandma called me "Miss America" and spoiled me rotten. I would go to day camp in Baltimore near her house that summer and make new friends. I was going to have so much fun, my mother said.

On the day that I was to leave Los Angeles in June of 1974, my nanny packed my brand-new, size 6x summer clothes into a suitcase, with my blankie tucked away safely inside. It was white with the letters of the alphabet and corresponding animals printed on it. I couldn't sleep without my blankie, which was well loved and tattered by this point. Truth be told, I still have it. It's now folded up in a safe place in my closet, and I find comfort knowing it's there.

My mother drove me to the airport on that June day. We headed down the familiar route down Laurel Canyon Boulevard, past the Country Store, until it turned into Crescent Heights Boulevard. Then it was on to La Cienega Boulevard all the way down to Los Angeles International Airport.

I'd flown out of LAX before, when my mother brought me to England in 1971 to record *The Road Is No Place for a Lady*, her second record for RCA as a solo artist, at the world-famous Trident Studios. She made a habit of bringing me along on work trips whenever she could. I'd also been to the arrivals section of LAX several times to pick her up when she would return from traveling for work. On one of those occasions, my nanny and I had been waiting for my mom to arrive, when I spotted her walking out of the baggage claim area onto the sidewalk. She was wearing one of her characteristic flowered, floor-length caftans, with a big floppy hat and her aviator sunglasses. Released from my nanny's grip, I ran as fast as I could toward my mom, who crouched down and threw her arms open wide to receive me.

Unfortunately, I wasn't the only person who had spotted my mom coming out of those airport doors. As I was approaching her running at nearly full speed, a man with long dark hair stepped directly into my path and asked her for her autograph. I slowed down and stopped in my tracks. Even at that young age, I understood that people admired my mom and wanted to talk to her, that they were important to her, and that it was part of her job to be nice to them. I also knew that I would have my turn with her as soon as she was done with them, and I knew to wait. Then I would get my hug and kiss.

On this day in 1974 my mother took my small hand in hers and led us through airport security and down to my plane's departure gate. We sat and waited until my flight was announced and we were called up to preboard, since I was traveling alone. Grandma was going to meet me on the other end, but it was my first time flying by myself. We talked about the things I would do at camp. "You're going to learn how to swim better, and then you can show me when we get home," she said. She wrapped her arms around me and gave me a big squeeze. Her bracelets jangled, making their familiar, comforting sound.

Soon the time came for me to board. My mom led me onto the plane and helped me find my seat. She buckled me in and kissed both my cheeks repeatedly. Left-right, left-right, left-right. "I'm going to miss you *so much*. I'm going to think about you every single minute of every single day," she whispered in my ear. "I love you so much."

She reminded me of the things that we would do together at the end of the summer when she returned. I was going to start at a new school, and she would be home for a while so we could spend uninterrupted time together.

"The time is going to fly by," she promised. "You're not even gonna notice. You'll be so busy at camp and with Grandma. She might even take you to Florida to see Bubby and Ben. And before you even know it, we'll be together again."

She gave me a last hug and kiss goodbye and started making her way down the airplane aisle. Taking just a few steps, she turned and looked back at me.

"Don't forget to look out your window. I'll be right there in the airport window, waving at you. Look for me," she said, and I did.

A few minutes later she was there at the terminal window, waving frantically at the plane. I waved back, hoping that she'd see me. I wasn't convinced that she could but even now, especially now, I hope she did. Because that was the last time I saw her—and the last time she saw me—through that airport terminal window, waving goodbye.

———■———

My memories of childhood are not numerous, but they're vivid. I've thought about that last goodbye, nearly fifty years ago, many times since then. I can remember the details as if they happened yesterday. And I'd rather hold on to that image of my mother than the one that others tried to superimpose on her final days. Because when she died, a stupid rumor circulated about her cause of death, and a certain ham sandwich turned into an urban legend.

I knew there had to be more to this story. After she was found lifeless in her bedroom in London on July 29, 1974, the official autopsy report revealed that the cause of her death had nothing to do with choking or with food. Her heart had stopped beating in her sleep. She'd had a heart attack.

There had to be a reason *why* such a rumor would circulate in the first place. I could feel it in my bones. I made it my mission to figure out why. I had to for my own edification. I needed to separate my mother from that myth and all the others that swirled around her, to discern fact from fiction. Because only then could I learn who she truly was and, in turn, who I am, not just as her daughter but as a woman in this world.

Challenging authority and asking questions are behaviors that were common among all the women who preceded me. We inherited them from my great-grandmother Chaya, who had the guts to leave Poland and sail to America on her own in 1914.

That alone takes serious courage. And perseverance. And an instinct for survival.

When I first considered writing this book, I asked my great-aunt Lil, Chaya's youngest child, to tell me about my mom. Lil was ninety at the time. I shared my desire to learn the truth about my mother's life and death and to write her story, the story she didn't get a chance to write herself.

Lil's immediate response was, "What the hell do you know about her? You were too young."

"Exactly," I said. "That's the point."

Saturday, July 27

Dearest Owenski,

I'm really sorry I haven't written to you in such a long time. I guess the only excuse I can offer is that I have been busier since I got here than I have ever, ever been. My work schedule is much harder here than it ever is when we are at home.

I am writing this letter in my dressing room at the theatre, between shows. The name of the theatre is The Palladium. It is the most famous theatre in England. Also, it is really beautiful. It has lovely green carpets and gold lamps. When the hall is full, there are nearly two and a half thousand people. My dressing room is very nice. It doesn't have green carpets or gold lamps, but it is comfortable. I spend at least five hours here every day. I arrive here at around 5:30 in the evening and leave at midnight. And, because I do two shows every night, I must wash and

set my hair between shows. Then , after
the second show I'm usually so tired
that I go straight back to the apartment
where George and I are staying, and I
go right to sleep.

But, besides the fact that I miss you,
so much and wish we were together right
now, this minute, I feel good just knowing
that you are with Ma Bess, who loves you
very much. I also know that you are
having a good time at camp and you will
have so many things to tell me when I get
home.

I tried to telephone you today, but I
guess the number I have for Bubby and
Ben in florida must not be correct.

Anyway, my darling child, I love, love,
love you and miss you lots. I'll write
again soon.

I send you a big hug and lots of
kisses.

All my love, and we'll be together
soon.

Love - Mommy

My Mama, Cass

CHAPTER 1

MY MOTHER ARRIVED AT LONDON'S HEATHROW Airport in mid-June 1974 in her big, round dark sunglasses, with her tennis racket tucked under one arm and a beautiful gold-handled cane grasped in her other hand. She was still recovering from knee surgery after slipping on some water on our kitchen floor at home in the Hollywood Hills. But here she was in London, where she was booked for twenty-eight shows from July 15 through July 27 at the Palladium, performing two shows a day. Rehearsals had already taken place in Los Angeles in the weeks preceding her voyage across the pond, and she was as ready as she was going to be for these live performances when she arrived.

Her costumes for the sold-out shows had been designed by Bob Mackie, who was famous for his use of sequins. For her opening show, he'd created a red sequined gown with large bell-shaped sleeves for her to wear. Around the neckline and the hemline of the sleeves, the dress was adorned with large gem-shaped rhinestones. It weighed more than twenty-five pounds. I can't imagine how she was even able to walk in that dress, let alone perform for hours. When she came off stage that first night, she handed it to her manager, Allan Carr, and declared, "I'm never wearing this dress again!" and she meant it. She never wore it again.

Two weeks of shows at the Palladium concluded with a final performance on July 27. Later that night, Mick Jagger's thirty-first birthday party was being held, and my mom had been invited. The party would have been a hot ticket in London, filled with celebrities and lots of her friends, and she would stay there all night partying with the crowd. But before leaving her dressing room she stopped to leave a note for Debbie Reynolds, who was the next performer to be playing the Palladium. With a tube of lipstick, she scrawled across the dressing room mirror: "If they are half as nice to you as they were to me, you'll have the time of your life."

I imagine that after her twenty-eighth sold-out Palladium show, my mom must have been exhausted. She also must have felt on top of the world, having finally experienced success as a solo artist and not simply as Mama Cass of the Mamas and the Papas. I know she must have been happy. That thought has been one of my main comforts as the years have gone by.

My mother returned to her rented London flat late in the afternoon on July 28 after attending a tea that had been held in her honor. She was tired and hungry. Her friend Joe Croyle, one of the dancers from the show who was also staying with her at the flat, looked in the refrigerator but found only sliced ham, some cheese, some bread, and a Coca-Cola. He made my mother a sandwich, poured her some Coke, and left the food on a side table in her bedroom while my mom ran her bath. Afterward, she got into bed with the TV on, leaving her bedroom door slightly open.

Joe went out for the evening, returning in the early morning to find my mom's door still ajar, her TV still on, and the sound of her snoring.

The next day, more than eighteen hours after she'd gone to bed, my mother still wasn't awake. Her personal assistant, Dot, became increasingly concerned and asked George Caldwell, my mother's road manager and sometimes boyfriend, to check on her. George refused to go into the room, which Dot found unusual, considering they were supposedly a couple. So Dot went into the room herself and saw my mother lying on the bed naked. She immediately felt uncomfortable, even though as my mother's assistant she'd seen her without clothes on many times before. But this time, something just didn't feel right, Dot later told me. She insisted that George come in to take a look. A few minutes later, he returned to the living room.

"We've got a problem," he said. "Cass is dead."

That same day, on the other side of the Atlantic, I was in the middle of an otherwise ordinary afternoon at summer camp in Baltimore. I'd become an underwater swimming champion that summer, able to travel from the shallow end of the pool to the deep end without once surfacing for air. One of the counselors came and found me practicing in the pool. "Your grandma called," she said when I came up for air. "She's at home waiting for you. I'm going to give you a ride there."

When I walked into the apartment, my grandmother was sitting at the dining room table with a big glass ashtray and her cigarettes and lighter resting in front of her. She asked me to sit down. I did.

"Honey, your mom isn't coming home," she said. "She died." Grandma Bess wasn't known for beating around the bush.

In the long silence that followed I thought that Grandma must have made a mistake. *This can't be right.* I told myself. *Mom always comes back. She always does when she's been working.*

"OK," I said, wanting the conversation to be over. I stood up and left the table abruptly. I was numb and confused. *What did she mean, that my mother wasn't going to come home?* Nothing made any sense.

To lose a mother when you're only seven is to lose everything familiar and known. In my case, even more so. As a single parent, my mom was both mother *and* father to me. My biological father had never been a part of our family structure. I didn't even know his name. I didn't even really know what a dad was or did, as I had no model for one. So when my mom died, I felt totally alone, as if I were now completely on my own and would have to learn to take care of myself.

The women in my family are all total badasses. Smart, educated, determined, cantankerous, driven nonconformists. They don't take no for an answer. They all have incredible constitutions, and it takes a lot to get them down. My mother was cut from the same cloth. I'd like to count myself among these amazing women, all survivors for one reason or another.

Their lessons must have been deeply embedded in my DNA. Even at seven, I knew I would have to start tapping into those skills in order to survive.

Everyone has an origin story. My mother's begins in a middle-class Jewish family in post–World War II Baltimore. The circumstances that brought Chaya to the United States in 1914 vary slightly, depending on which family member is telling the story. The version I heard from Grandma Bess, Chaya's eldest child, is the one I know best and the one I stand by.

Bess's mother, Chaya, had fallen in love with a local boy in Ostrołęka, Poland, where her father was a cantor in the local synagogue. Chaya wanted very much to marry the boy, but they were from different sides of the tracks, so to speak, and the union was unsupported by the families. Grandma Bess couldn't remember which of the two had been from the "wrong side," but it ended up that Chaya went off to the US to "make her fortune," as Grandma told me.

When she'd earned enough money, she returned to Poland to marry her sweetheart, only to discover he hadn't patiently waited for her return and had married someone else.

Heartbroken, Chaya returned to the US and to the more comfortable life that she had created there. She entered into an
arranged marriage with a man named Joseph Levine, a tailor
by trade, who had also immigrated from Poland. Together they
had three daughters. They moved frequently, from California
to Pennsylvania and finally to New York, with each subsequent
daughter born in a different city. Grandma Bess, the eldest,
was born in San Francisco in November 1915.

My great-grandparents went on to have two more daughters, Julia (not sure what year she was born) and, finally, Lillian
in 1919. All three of the Levine daughters shared their mother's
perseverance, and all three were strong independent-minded
women. And those three sisters each had like-minded, spir-
ited daughters. Those daughters became lawyers, teachers, and
rock stars, and eventually some of those women had daughters
of their own. We are all descended from this woman, Chaya
Leyzor.

As Adolf Hitler ravaged his way through Poland, his Nazi
troops invaded the shtetl of Ostrołęnka, killing all of the Jewish people who lived there. The Leyzor family that remained
in Poland perished. There had been six siblings in the family, three boys and three girls. Chaya was the middle daughter, and both she and her younger sister had been sent away
from Poland a few years earlier to be married off. They were
some of the few members of the family that survived. The
pain that this must have caused Chaya, Bubby, as I called her,

is unimaginable. By then, she had already raised her girls and was even a grandparent to my own mother, who had been born in 1941. Bubby lost her entire family in one fell swoop. How can someone begin to make sense of such horror? How does someone experiencing that level of grief continue to put one foot in front of the other every single day—and somehow be okay? How was she not depressed beyond measure? All that I know is that she *did it*. She persevered because that's what she knew how to do.

When the Holocaust Memorial Museum opened in Washington, DC, in 1993, Bubby had been gone for over a decade. Invitations were issued to the families of survivors. One of our cousins, Batya, was in attendance. During the presentation, representatives from the various villages stood on stage holding signs with the names of their villages. Batya approached the Ostrołęnka representative, who recalled details of the horrific day of the Nazi invasion. It's deeply painful to recount what was learned of my family's fate there. It's important to know that the Jews of Ostrołęnka were marched into the woods, forced to dig their own graves, and buried alive. I'm so grateful that Bubby never knew that. I do know she carried a great sense of responsibility for leaving her family and coming to America and not staying and perishing alongside them. Cousins who spent time with Bubby toward the end of her life in a retirement home in New Jersey said that in one breath, she'd speak happily of never having to cook another meal, and in the next breath, she would be in tears. When asked why she was crying, Bubby replied that she should have died with her family in Poland. My cousins tried to reassure her that she was meant to come here to America; that if she hadn't gotten on that boat and gone across the ocean, none of us would be here. I hope that that knowledge brought her some joy.

My grandmother Bessie Levine, the eldest of the three daughters, became a teacher after graduating from high school. One night she was visiting a friend's apartment in preparation for an evening out. While primping in the bathroom, she heard the apartment door open, and then close. She heard footsteps in the living room and then the sound of a man whistling. The tune was her favorite opera aria. Intrigued, she went to investigate. And there stood my handsome grandfather, Philip Cohen, the youngest of thirteen children in an Orthodox Jewish family.

Bessie and Philip fell in love and married within a few weeks that November of 1940, even though my grandmother was technically engaged to someone else, whom she left "standing at the altar," as she told the story. Bess and Philip were absolutely wild for one another and shared a love for song. Both had incredibly beautiful singing voices, and that passion turned into a gift they gave their three children.

My mom, Ellen Naomi Cohen, was born on September 19, 1941, in Baltimore, Maryland, with a head full of dark hair. Her parents adored her, and by all accounts, she was a happy little girl. For the first seven years of her life, she was the center of their attention.

Grandma Bess loved to tell me stories about my mother's childhood as I grew up without her. She said that my mom could walk into a room that was "neat as a pin" and it would literally fall apart around her. Apparently, my mother tended to be on the messier side as an adult, too, never keeping her possessions organized. Michelle Phillips, my mom's bandmate, the other mama in the Mamas and the Papas told me about a time she'd gone to my mom's apartment in Hollywood to see her, but my mother wasn't home when Michelle arrived. The place was a wreck, according to Michelle, complete with an industrial-sized plastic jug of mayonnaise upside down on the floor, the contents everywhere. Michelle cleaned up the mess and left. I wonder how long the room took to revert to its previous condition of chaos after that overhaul from Michelle.

Grandma also told me about a time that she took my mother to the library, something they would do together before the other two Cohen children were born. That would have made mom four or five at the time, certainly before school age. At the library, my grandmother got my mother settled in the children's area and walked away to find whatever she wanted to look at that day. Before long she heard my mother's voice wailing across the quiet library. "You lied to me! You. Lied. TO. ME!!!!" She cried plaintively and louder with every word. Grandma rushed over. My mom was sitting on the floor with an encyclopedia open on her small lap.

"You lied to meeeeeee!" she cried out, her little finger pointing to an illustration depicting a tree with paper money hanging from its branches like fruit. The Cohens were a working-class family, and my mom had been told repeatedly that money didn't just grow on trees. Yet, here was proof that it did. A money tree. Oh, the insult.

The age of seven is a recurring theme in my mother's story and, later, in mine. My mom was seven years old when her grandfather was found dead in a motel room, sans wallet and valuables. As the story goes, he had been entertaining a "professional" who apparently absconded with said wallet and left him there. Whether his death was a murder or from natural causes depends on which family member you ask.

I'm not certain, but I think it's fair to say that the marriage between Chaya and Joseph wasn't a loving or passionate relationship at that point. Maybe it had never been, as it had been arranged for convenience so many years prior. Many years after Joseph died, Chaya married a wonderful man named Ben Benowitz. I knew them as Bubby and Ben. Bubby finally found love in her life the second time around, and they stayed together until she died in 1980.

My mom was also almost seven years old when her parents prepared to welcome a new baby, their second child. Unfortunately, just before the birth, my mom contracted a nasty case of ringworm, which was contagious. In light of the baby's impending arrival, it was determined that it would be safest to send my mom to live with her grandparents for a while. Chaya and Joseph adored their granddaughter and spoiled her with love and attention, and also with the bountiful amounts of food that Chaya prepared. My aunt Leah remembers that Bubby had an "almost pathological need" to feed people. Given that she lived through the Great Depression, this isn't surprising.

Being sent away from home may have had more of an effect on my mother's young mind than anyone had anticipated. As she revealed to *Ladies' Home Journal* in March of 1969, "I was a thin child and a poor eater until my sister Leah was born when I was almost seven years old. I imagine that aroused some insecurities within me. At least so I've discovered through psychoanalysis. After Leah came along, I did the thing that was most acceptable to me—and what I thought would please my parents—eat. By the time I dropped out of high school, two weeks before graduation, I weighed 180 pounds." Gaining and losing weight would become a pattern for the rest of my mom's life.

Four years after my aunt Leah's birth, my uncle Joe was born. His birth in May of 1952 completed the Cohen family unit.

My grandfather Philip was somewhat of an entrepreneur, and at one point he even owned a deli in Washington, DC, that JFK had been known to frequent. Philip was well-known and beloved in the community and liked to joke around. He would refer to his regular customers with silly nicknames, calling tall people "Shorty," or perhaps if you were on the heavier side, he might have called you "Slim."

When Uncle Joe was a little boy, he had asthma and was a bit sickly. He was always on the skinny, smaller side. *Bonanza* was a popular television show at the time, and my grandfather began referring to Joey as "Hoss" after the big burly character on the show. "Hoss" became Uncle Joe's family nickname from that point onward. Philip also had a nickname for my mom, whom he called Cassandra. The name stuck with her for the rest of her life, too, and she would later become known to the world as Cass.

After the deli closed for good, my grandfather continued to go to the weekly auctions that were held for restaurant supplies. Besides equipment, one could get a fantastic bargain on various goods necessary for the food service business, including deep discounts on canned foods. One day after returning from one of these auctions, he told my grandmother he'd bought a bus. A bus that didn't run, he told her. She thought he was crazy, but he had a plan. He took all of the seats out of the bus and installed a kitchen. Then, he had the bus towed to locations where construction was taking place and set about feeding the workers. In effect, he had created Baltimore's first food truck.

It was expected that every family member would pitch in and work on the bus to keep the operation running. My mom did early morning shifts before school and in the afternoons. The bus was towed to various worksites, to malls under construction, and to Washington, DC, in 1958, where the Museum of History and Technology, now known as the National Museum of American History, was being built. Breakfast and lunch were served daily to hungry construction workers at the museum site.

My grandparents were both hard workers, putting in long hours that essentially turned their children into latchkey kids before the term was even invented. My mother, as the eldest, was responsible for her two younger siblings. As she would later tell *Rolling Stone*, "I remember when I was ten years old in Washington, DC, and I lived with the fear of the atom bomb that would keep me awake nights and make me wake up screaming. I used to babysit for my younger brother and sister, and I'd be terrified if I heard a siren, a police car or an ambulance. I'd say, 'My god, what if this is it! How do I protect them?'"

My grandparents were also forward thinkers who didn't necessarily go along with society's mainstream ideas. They believed in socialism. They included the kids in discussions of current events at meals and were always interested in their opinions. Their house was always filled with lively and intelligent conversation. By the time my mother was old enough to understand the adults, she was asking pointed questions— questions that a child normally wouldn't have shown interest in. My aunt Lil, Grandma's sister, remembered how my mother as a very young child once asked a doctor friend of the family what he thought of the "world situation." His mind was blown by her, according to Aunt Lil.

Music was a constant presence in the Cohen household. My grandmother played the piano and possessed a beautiful alto voice, and my grandfather had a rich tenor. Gathering together around the piano, listening to music, and singing along was something that they did frequently as a family. Leah remembers singing the Patience and Prudence song "Tonight You Belong to Me" with my mom when they were about nine and sixteen.

Though I never heard them sing together, I can imagine how magical they must have sounded. When people of the same genetic origin sing together, they create a perfect blend, unlike any other. There is often a certain *similarity* to those voices. And in our family, Leah calls it the Cohen Honk. Musical history has given us examples of this in the Lennon Sisters; the sisters known as Heart, Ann and Nancy Wilson; and of course, my personal favorite, sisters Carnie and Wendy Wilson of Wilson Phillips. Families just sound great together.

CHAPTER 2

THE COHEN FAMILY MOVED FROM HOME TO HOME within Washington, Baltimore, and Alexandria, Virginia, during the 1950s, which meant the three kids changed schools frequently. When the family moved once more from Virginia back to Maryland, my mom enrolled at Forest Park High School, a large public high school in the Dorchester neighborhood of northwest Baltimore.

Most mornings she was waking at the crack of dawn to work on the bus with her dad and was often late to school, which didn't please the administration. Socially, she didn't have an easy time of it, either.

Rona Weintraub, a high school girlfriend of my mom's at Forest Park High School, remembers that at the time, students graduated twice a year: in winter and in late spring. My mom graduated in February of 1960 and Rona graduated that June, which meant they weren't in classes together. They were, however, in the same sorority.

Being part of a sorority was all important to high school girls in the early sixties, as it represented social stature. My mom knew this all too well. She arrived at Forest Park with a Sigma Pi Sigma sorority pin from her previous high school affixed to her sweater. The pin guaranteed automatic acceptance into the sorority at any school that had a chapter.

The Sigmas at Forest Park were less than welcoming to this new student in their midst, but they had little choice but to accept her into their fold. My mom didn't necessarily fit the Sigma Pi image, which was to be fashionably dressed and slender. Early in her high school career, she had begun wearing baggy dresses with her knee socks sagging down around her ankles to the rims of her saddle shoes. Her fingernails were bitten down to the quick. Being overweight in high school was no walk in the park. She learned that the best way to deal with the unkind things other kids said to her was with humor and her caustic wit. Not to mention her creativity.

Sigma Pi Sigma held sorority rush teas every year, where members would meet prospective new sisters and decide who would be invited to join their group. "She [Cass] would create the whole thing for us," Rona remembers. "She would teach us the song, and maybe a little dance that went along with it, or some kind of a skit. She would rehearse with us, and then she would disappear. She wouldn't be out in the front when the prospective members were coming to meet us." When I ask Rona why this was, she says it was because my mom *knew* the other Sigma Pis were embarrassed by her, and so she chose not to have prospective new members see her.

It hurts me to hear this, to know that my mother quietly acknowledged what the other girls thought of her and felt she had to act on it. But did she really accept it? She told anyone who would listen that one day she was going to be the most famous fat girl who ever lived. She was convinced of it. She even told Rona, at the lunch table in the cafeteria, how she planned to take on a stage name. She would take her initials, E. C. (Ellen Cohen), and reverse them to C. E. She would then call herself Cass for her first name, as a nod to her father's nickname for her, Cassandra. My mom later told me that the last name Elliot was in memory of a good friend who had died in a car accident in high school. Cass Elliot. That would be her new name. I think that it's incredibly cool of my mom to know and to verbalize what she was dreaming of becoming at such a young age, and then to make it happen for herself, despite the many early obstacles life threw in her way. She persevered, like the little engine that could. She definitely thought she could, and as it turned out, she sure as hell *did* become one of the most famous fat girls to ever live.

As my mom continued to gain weight throughout high school, her parents became more and more concerned. They did the only thing that they knew to do: they consulted the family doctor. He placed my mom on an amphetamine. The drug had been used as an appetite suppressant with some success and was widely prescribed as such at the time.

The physical dangers of introducing amphetamines to a still developing human brain wouldn't be known for decades. Now it's known to be linked to eventual heart disease, addiction, and substance abuse. Emotionally, the message I fear my mom may have gotten could have been, *You're overweight, so something must be wrong with you. Take this pill. It will fix the problem.* The thought that something is wrong with you is bad enough, but the idea that a pill or drug might fix you can be even more dangerous.

The amphetamine made my mother antsy and unable to pay attention in school. It also didn't help her lose any weight, and my grandparents became more concerned as my mom continued to struggle. They arranged for her to see a psychologist, which was not something that was done often as an outpatient in those days. Being encouraged to identify one's feelings and talking openly about them was still very new in the early 1960s.

It was right about this time that my mom took her first decisive step as a performer. In 1973, she told the story to Skitch Henderson, the former bandleader for *The Tonight Show* who'd turned radio host for the US Army Reserve Radio. The interview took place as they sat in a "sumptuous and humidified suite," according to Henderson, when my mom was in Las Vegas for an engagement at the Flamingo Hilton.

"Cass, where did it begin with you?" he asked.

"Oh, dear," she sighed, before continuing, "I guess it really began between my junior and senior year of high school."

"What did it?" he interrupted. "There must have been a springboard."

"Well, my best friend at the time. I was studying French in night school, because I'd had four years of Latin and needed two languages to get into college. And my best girlfriend was doing summer stock that summer and when I finished my classes I'd go out and pick her up," she began.

"The play was *The Boyfriend*, and it was well received. Its run had just been extended. One of the girls in the chorus had made a commitment to go onto another show, so she couldn't stay. One night I went to pick up her friend after the show, and the production was desperately looking around for somebody to replace the chorus member."

"My girlfriend said, 'Well, *she* sings!!'" my mom said, laughing. "And I had braces on my teeth, and you know, just every other adolescent hangup, and the next thing I knew I was in the chorus!" She did the show for three weeks and then went back to school, but somehow, high school didn't seem the same to her anymore. Her parents wanted her to become a doctor, the ultimate Jewish parents' dream, but this idea was becoming less and less appealing to her.

"So, I talked it over with my parents, and I said, 'Listen, I'd like to be in show business,'" she continued, "and they laughed. 'Haha. Funny joke,' they said, 'Nobody's going to pay you for that, and don't be silly. Go to college like you're supposed to.' I said, 'Well, look, I'll make a deal with you. Give me five years, and I'll go to New York and try to make something of myself. If I don't make it in five years, I'll come back.'"

In the winter of 1960, my mom moved to New York City to pursue her dream of being on Broadway. She would stay with her aunt Lil, Lil's husband, Jack, and their school-aged daughter, Ralfee, on Riverside Drive near 125th Street. Driving into New York, and not realizing the dangers of the big city, she parked her car stuffed full of all her belongings at the curb, unlocked. When she returned, everything was gone including the car. Everything. The family rallied to replace what she'd lost and managed to pull together the things that she needed to get started in New York. Losing all of her stuff must have been awful for her. I'd surely have been a wreck. It was around this time that my mother fully adopted her stage name in place of the Jewish-sounding name that she'd been given at birth.

When I turned eighteen and became responsible for handling my mother's estate, I became weary of explaining over and over again why my last name was different from hers. I adopted Elliot as a legal alias to make things easier for myself. Later, when I got married, I added my new husband's name to the mix, making my name Owen Elliot-Kugell.

But I'm getting ahead of myself, bouncing between things that happened in my mother's life and my own. So many stories began in her life, and then continued into mine to reach their conclusions. Questions asked in her lifetime receive their answers in mine.

In New York City, my mom began to audition for any production she heard about off and on Broadway. In the meantime, she landed a job as a coat checker at a local club to make some money. One afternoon that following spring, my mom was at the apartment alone. She opened the windows to let in some fresh air, singing loudly as she straightened up the apartment. Ralfee arrived home from school and burst through the door, indignantly informing my mom that she could be heard singing all the way down at the corner. Ralfee was mortified, but my mother was ecstatic. "Great!" she said. "That's what I was hoping for!"

Mom tucked many, many auditions and many, many rejections under her belt, reportedly losing the part of Miss Marmelstein in *I Can Get It for You Wholesale* to another up-and-coming young Jewish actress and singer, Barbra Streisand, who was auditioning in New York City at the same time. My mother remarked to her friends at the time that "there just don't seem to be many parts for a 200-pound ingenue."

In March of 1962, my grandfather Philip was involved in a minor car accident. Although he appeared to be unhurt at the time, his abdomen had been thrust forward into the steering wheel. Before long, he was in pain, and was admitted to a hospital in Virginia, where tests were done. It was determined that he needed further medical attention. He was transferred to Baltimore, where one of his older brothers was a doctor, and exploratory surgery was performed.

My grandfather Philip died from a heart attack soon after the surgery. The cause of his abdominal pain was never officially discovered, but Leah recalls being told that he had died of pancreatitis, and since the pancreas is located in the region of his abdominal trauma, that may have been the case.

The family was understandably devastated. At the funeral, the chapel was packed full of people who came to pay tribute. My grandfather had always been a good man, the kind of restaurant owner who had never turned away a hungry customer who couldn't pay his bill. His kindness and the love of so many in his community was shown to our family that day in the copious amount of people who came to pay their respects.

After the funeral, the family sat together in the rented limousine, following the black Cadillac hearse to the cemetery. The mood was somber, and everyone was quiet until my mom spoke up.

"Well, at least Dad finally got to ride in the frigging Cadillac the same year," she said.

As Leah, who was thirteen at the time, recalls, "Our dad had always really wanted to drive a brand-new Cadillac. He thought they were the coolest cars. I just remember us all cracking up and for a moment thinking, *Is this OK? To be laughing while you're at your dad's funeral?* I mean, there's no question we were all bereft *beyond* belief and I remember saying something like, 'Should we be laughing?' and my sister said, 'Daddy would want us to.' And he would have. It's really true. He wouldn't have wanted us to sit around moping."

After her husband died, my grandma Bess became the family's sole provider, working long hours to provide for Leah and Joey, who was only ten. My mom felt drawn back home to help take care of her younger siblings while Grandma worked, but she stayed only until late June when she left to join the tour of *The Music Man*, which she'd auditioned for that spring for the Pocono Playhouse.

Myrna Van Buren, now in her nineties, was the choreographer for the show and still remembers my mom's audition. "Her voice was unbelievable," she tells me on a call from her home in Northern California. "That was the reason she was cast, having no experience in theater. She had comedic timing, oh yes. It wasn't only the voice we needed, but you needed to be able to move, to dance, to take instruction on specific dance steps, because she and the mayor had to do a dance together. Yes, we knew there was something special about her."

"What role was she cast in?" I asked.

"It was called the role of the fat girl," Myrna recalls.

The role of the fat girl? I groaned externally as well as internally. That would never happen today, but knowing the context of those times, the times in which my mother had to get her start, I can appreciate even more the obstacles and prejudices she had to face on an ongoing basis.

The tour of *The Music Man* took the cast and crew through the northern parts of New England and into Massachusetts and upstate New York. They were on the road for ten weeks and were very well received, according to Myrna. When the tour was over, my mom moved back home, into the basement of the house her mom had bought in Alexandria, Virginia. It must have felt nice to be at home with the family again. I'm sure that Grandma was also glad to have all three of her kids home with her. However, Leah was having a difficult time after her father died, and her grades began to falter. When a very progressive coed boarding school up in the Berkshires offered her a scholarship, she enrolled there for her eleventh-grade year.

My mom started classes at American University in Washington, DC, on a provisional basis, based on her high school grades and test scores. She hadn't received her diploma yet and wouldn't receive it officially for another eleven years.

As a twenty-one-year-old college freshman in the fall of 1962, my mom was older than most of her classmates. Out of sync with the other students, she spent much of her non-class time in the folk clubs in Georgetown. She'd been in college for only about six weeks when she met a man named Tim Rose, an extraordinary guitar and banjo player with a gravelly voice. Tim had recently returned from a stint in the US Air Force and was looking for musicians to jam with to create a new sound. My mom would later refer to Tim as the person who "made me a star."

A mutual friend pointed my mom out to Tim at a club where she was singing. "I looked over and there was this very *huge* woman sitting there," Tim later recalled in *Dream a Little Dream of Me: The Life of Cass Elliot*, Eddi Fiegel's 2005 biography of my mom. "I very unkindly turned to our mutual friend, 'Look, I don't care what she sings like, I was envisioning Mary Travers. This is not what I was expecting.' The friend replied, 'Then you're in for a real surprise. Just listen.'"

Then my mom began to sing.

Duly impressed by what he heard, Tim went and introduced himself, and after five minutes of conversation he was enchanted. They began singing folk tunes together, with Tim on the guitar and mom singing the parts he directed her to. Pretty soon they began to have a groove going. "I know a guy in Chicago, why don't we go to Chicago?" my mother later recalled Tim saying to her. Everything seemed to be returning to normal at home in Alexandria, under the circumstances. So, my mom took her savings and bought an ancient Volkswagen Beetle, and off to Chicago she went with Tim to try out the friend who was interested in making their duo a trio.

It was now wintertime, and as cold as winters in Chicago can get. In the introduction to her 1973 album, *Don't Call Me Mama Anymore*, which was recorded live at the famed Mister Kelly's nightclub in Chicago, my mom shared that Chicago was very special to her and explained why.

"We came to Chicago," she said, referring to that trip in 1962, "and it was very, very cold. About twenty-five below zero, and I did not have a coat. We worked at places like the Fickle Pickle, the Rising Moon, Old Town North. Places like that. Those places were at the time were what you called 'basket houses' and you would sing and maybe a couple other performers would sing also, and they would pass the basket and people would put in money. You would split it up, and if you made six dollars that was a BIG night."

Tim and my mom shared a one-bedroom apartment while rehearsing with Tim's friend John Brown. My mother took the bedroom and Tim slept in the cold living room. Together, the three of them formed a group, and soon booked a gig at a club in Omaha, Nebraska.

Unbeknownst to them, their opening act in Omaha was a young, male solo singer-songwriter named James Hendricks. He was handsome and talented, and I imagine my mother becoming completely besotted by him.

Jim was, and still is, a true Southern gentleman. I can practically hear him blushing over the phone when he recalls this part of the story. While he could just tell by the way my mom looked at him that she had a little crush on him, he tells me although he adored her it wasn't like *that* for him. Still, he had a beautiful voice, and John Brown really just wanted to go home to his wife and kids in Chicago. This substitution could work out just fine, in my mother's mind. She and Tim proposed the idea to Jim, who accepted wholeheartedly.

John headed home and the new trio returned to Alexandria, where they named themselves the Triumvirate and rehearsed and honed their act. They soon decided to head to Florida, where it was much warmer than Virginia.

"And so, we all piled into my Pontiac Tempest convertible," Jim recalls. "We went to Miami and sat on the beach and rehearsed all the stuff we wanted to sing." These songs would later appear on their first album, but that wouldn't happen for months. After seven or eight days, the group returned to Alexandria. Tim had a contact with a man named Bob Cavallo, who ran the Shadows, a key folk venue in nearby Washington, DC.

The group auditioned at the club for Cavallo, who was unimpressed. However, a talent manager named Roy Silver was also in the club at the time. Silver was currently representing the main headliner of the Shadows, a comedian named Bill Cosby.

Unlike Cavallo, Silver *was* impressed by what he saw that day. He called Tim the following day and asked how soon the group could be in New York City. He also told him he hated the name the Triumvirate, and that from then on, they would be known as the Big 3. Back in New York, Silver was responsible for booking acts at the Bitter End in Greenwich Village, and he booked the Big 3 as the headlining act for that summer of 1963.

The monthslong gig came complete with meager living accommodations above the club. There were two rooms, my mom in one and Tim and Jim in the other. The Village was chock full of coffee houses at the time, basket house after basket house where often the only payments the artists received came from donations from the crowd.

Also in New York that summer was Denny Doherty, a young tenor from Nova Scotia, Canada, performing with his folk group, the Halifax Three. Denny's pal Zalman Yanovsky, also from Canada, was in the group with him, and they had begun to make a name for themselves in New York City's burgeoning folk scene. As Denny recalled in his 2003 off-Broadway play, *Dream a Little Dream*, "I remember walking down Bleecker Street one night and this sound was coming out of the Bitter End—right through the brick walls. Cass Elliot and the Big 3.

"The first thing you noticed about Cass was her face," he continued. "It was an amazing face: fast and funny and beautiful. She was a big, eat-the-world, pass-the-bourbon, soft kind of woman who came to New York to make it on Broadway.

"I finally got up the nerve to introduce myself to Cass at the Dugout, an infamous watering hole next to the Bitter End," he said. "Or maybe she introduced herself to me, I can't remember. But I do remember the night we met. She said, 'We're going to try to drink each other under the table, aren't we? So, let's get under the table and drink.' And that's what we did—under the red checkered tablecloth, in the sawdust with a bottle of Jack Daniel's Green Label."

And so began an intimate friendship with a remarkable musician and man that would last for the rest of my mother's life, and well into mine.

CHAPTER 3

ROY SILVER WHOLEHEARTEDLY BELIEVED IN THE
Big 3 and was able to get them under contract to FM
Records and into a recording studio relatively quickly. The
cover of their first record featured just the number three, drawn
in a geometric design.

Silver relied on his many connections to get the Big 3
booked on *The Danny Kaye Show* and *The Tonight Show*, but
unfortunately the record company failed to market and promote the album, and sales were disappointing.

To keep some money coming in, Roy booked the Big 3 on
one of the new traveling Hootenanny folk music tours that
was crisscrossing the country that year. The Hootenanny Folk
Festival Tour traveled across the upper Midwest, through
places like Sioux Falls and Minneapolis, while another tour,
the Hootenanny USA! tour, trekked across the lower Midwest
and the Southeast with a different set of acts.

As Denny later described in his one-man show, "The Hoo-tenanny tours were a spinoff from the TV series [*Hootenanny on ABC*]. You'd go out, six to ten acts on a bus, hit the circuit. Like the old Allen Freed rock and roll shows. We played some of the same venues. That fall the Big 3 headed north, up through Chicago. The Halifax Three? We were on a tour, down through the Deep South headed for Texas."

Also, on the Hootenanny Folk Festival Tour with the Big 3 that fall was a young David Crosby, who my mom had become friends with back in Greenwich Village. Crosby remembers the tour bus accommodations being less than comfortable, certainly not the type of luxurious tour buses that later became associated with cross-country music tours. Those fancy buses often have beds to sleep on and other comforts of home. That wasn't the case here. This was just a regular old school bus with a bench seat at the rear. As the only woman on the tour, my mother was given that back bench as a courtesy. She hung up a sheet as a curtain for privacy. What must it have been like to have been the only female on those long stretches of road, with no one to talk with, like girls do? It must have been a lonely time for her, in that respect.

Denny Doherty and The Halifax Three were on the southern leg of the tour along with another band called the New Journeymen. This band was also a folk trio, composed of a talented young man named John Phillips, his young bride, Michelle, and a banjo player named Marshall Brickman. The New Journeymen were the next-to-closing act, making fifteen hundred a week, as Denny recalled. The Halifax Three, by comparison, were earning three hundred a week.

All of these folk artists were still on tour on November 22, 1963, when the news came from Dallas that President Kennedy had been killed. Like most Americans, my mother was shocked and devastated. JFK's brutal assassination affected her so deeply that she sat in her space at the rear of the bus all the way back to New York, weeping the entire time. His death had occurred suddenly, like her own father's the previous year. Because her emotions around her father's death were still raw and exposed, I imagine JFK's assassination further inflamed them.

In December of that same year, the Vietnam War was escalating, and the US government began making arrangements for a draft of young American men. This news had the potential to rip the Big 3 apart. Tim was a US Air Force veteran, which made him exempt from a draft. However, Jim was not. If Jim were to be drafted, the group would need to disband.

My mom came up with a brilliant solution. She and Jim would get married to grant him the draft exemption he needed. Roy Silver agreed this was a good plan. And so my mother married her bandmate and friend Jim Hendricks on December 10, 1963, in front of a judge at a small, clandestine wedding ceremony back home in Alexandria, Virginia.

My mother and Jim weren't in love; they were in a band. Nevertheless, Jim tells me they had a good time with it, acting like a married couple with my mom shopping for clothes for her "husband." Their marriage remained in a secretive and platonic state; they never consummated it or told anyone besides Roy Silver, Jim says. Even their bandmate, Tim, as it turns out, found out only as the Big 3 disbanded.

My mom and Jim stayed married for years on paper, only divorcing in February of 1972, when Jim was to marry his longtime girlfriend, Vanessa. The convenience of this arrangement made it so that when I was born in 1967, although Jim wasn't my actual biological father, he was listed on my birth certificate as though he were. A marriage, even a paper one, seemingly made having a baby much easier for my mom. Choosing to become a single mother at that time was still very unusual and not considered socially acceptable. I was officially named Owen Vanessa Hendricks after my legal "father," setting me up for a lifetime of teasing as a child over whether my birth father was Jimi Hendrix. Seriously. It was a *thing*.

The question usually went something like this: "Why is your last name Hendricks when your mom was Cass Elliot?" How did they even *know* my mom was named Cass Elliot in the first place? From their parents, I suspect. Nevertheless, this was Los Angeles, and private school at that, where being the child of a celebrity is almost commonplace. These kids were relentless with me, asking me what my father's name was. "Is your dad Jimi *Hendrix*?" was the constant, jeering comment, to which I learned to respond by stating how obvious that must be, considering my certain resemblance to him. As my mother had also learned, humor is the best and sometimes only way to deal with a situation that's complicated and uncomfortable to explain.

Even still. When I call Jim Hendricks, I usually begin the conversation with, "Hi, Jim! It's your pretend daughter!"

But again, I'm getting ahead of myself. After the Hootenanny tours ended, my mom returned to New York City and settled back in her old stomping grounds of Greenwich Village, where plenty of her fellow musician friends and artists also lived, including Denny Doherty. Denny and my mom had stayed in touch throughout their different tours, often spending hours on the telephone at their respective stops. They'd become best friends and confidants along the way.

Also hanging around the Village at the time was a nineteen-year-old guitar player named John Sebastian. John had met my mother when the artist he had been accompanying, a blues singer named Valentine Pringle, shared the bill with the Big 3 one night at the Bitter End. As John remembers, he had just finished his show with Valentine and was heading downstairs to the dressing room area when he encountered the Big 3 heading up the stairs to the stage to perform. As my mom passed by John, he said she was "scatting the hell" out of one the songs that Valentine had just performed, complete with the blues stylings he'd just done. It cracked John up on the spot, and he was enamored from that moment on.

And so, on February 9, 1964, the night that the Beatles were scheduled to appear on the *Ed Sullivan Show*, my mom invited John over to watch the show at her apartment. "Ringo will be here," she told him. "You have to come." John didn't believe her, of course. How silly could that be? He agreed to come over anyway, and upon arriving knocked on her front door. It was opened by a tall man with long shaggy hair. Not quite Ringo, but someone who looked a little bit like him, John surmised. It was Zal Yanovsky of the Halifax Three. My mom had really wanted them to meet.

John didn't go anywhere without his guitar strapped to him in those days, and before long, he and Zal began to jam together. They seemed to be getting along well, and to keep the excitement up, my mom casually sidled over to Zal and murmured something to the effect that John had said how good a guitarist Zal was, and then vice versa, making each one feel the other's admiration without either of them actually having to say it out loud.

"It was like being in sixth grade and having someone tell you that someone *likes* you," John recalled. "She'd go and whisper in his ear, then come whisper in mine."

My mother would soon come to be known for her incredible, almost psychic intuition as it pertained to creatively pairing her various musician friends. She somehow knew who would sound good together and also get along famously as well. Denny used to refer to her as the "puppeteer," pulling the strings on the characters from behind the scenes.

And she was absolutely right this time. Bringing John Sebastian and Zal Yanovsky together on that February night in 1964 was a fateful introduction. As John Sebastian recalls,

"By pairing me and Zalman Yanovsky, she set the spark that created the Lovin' Spoonful." Along with bassist Steve Boone and drummer Joe Butler, the Lovin' Spoonful would go on to produce timeless hits like "Do You Believe in Magic?" and "Summer in the City."

In early 1964, the Big 3 headed back into the studio to record a second album, despite friction crackling between members around the direction the group should take. By the midsixties, music had begun to evolve from the popular American folk of the early part of the decade to a new type of sound. Rock and roll had been born, and instruments had evolved as well. The electric guitar replacing the acoustic guitar was one of the most notable changes. My mom wanted to incorporate some of these new sounds and styles into the Big 3, but Tim didn't share her vision. He liked what they had been doing and he didn't believe the change would be worth it.

The Big 3's second record was titled *The Big 3 Live in the Recording Studio*. The cover featured the three members with my mom in the middle with her head tipped back, smiling. Her dark hair was piled in a bun high on her head. She was dressed to the nines in a black dress replete with a modest white lace collar, designed by Jim Hendricks's girlfriend, Vanessa, who would later go on to design outfits for country music star Emmylou Harris. Tim and Jim posed in black suit jackets over starched white shirts and black bow ties. The three of them looked like respectable young people of the midsixties, more suited to an Upper East Side cocktail party than a Greenwich Village basket club.

The album included several standout performances, including my mom's vocal on the song "Wild Women (Don't Get the Blues)." The vaudeville style of the 1924 song by Ida Cox perfectly suited my mom's voice and persona. Her contralto was right out front, loud and clear, gravelly at all the right spots. She and Tim had worked out a new arrangement for the song, and she sang the *shit* out of it. I think it's one of the best vocals she ever recorded.

The album was released in June of 1964 but, just like the trio's previous release, was poorly marketed and promoted, and sales were again disappointing. Music was now going through a permanent transformation period—rock and roll and Motown were flooding the airwaves—and folk music was no longer as widely popular as it had been. In the summer of 1964, the Beatles, the Beach Boys, and the Supremes topped the music charts, and the Rolling Stones were poised to strike within a year. The Big 3, in its current form, had reached the end of its moment in time.

Additionally, Tim had finally been told of my mom and Jim's "marriage" and was duly annoyed. So, Jim and my mom went to Tim and told him the arrangement wasn't working for them anymore. They wanted out. He didn't disagree, and promptly decided to leave New York and take his act solo.

As the Big 3 was unraveling, another little group spontaneously started to take shape in New York. My mom and

Jim had been spending time with Denny and Zal of the now-defunct Halifax Three, and they'd all started singing together. Soon, they found themselves having unintentionally reinvented the Big 3 minus Tim, forming what became known as Cass Elliot and the Big 3. Though this time, the "3" were the three men, Jim, Denny, and Zal.

Before long, the foursome renamed themselves the Mugwumps, borrowing a nineteenth-century political term that describes someone who is undecided or neutral on a subject, with their "mug" on one side of the proverbial fence, and their "wump" on the other. For a group made up of three men and a woman, with a musical style that was one part folk music and one part rock and roll, the moniker fit them well.

Denny told the story like this: "I got the name from my Newfoundland Granny who was always saying, 'Ah, you're like a bloody mugwump sittin' on a fence with your mug on one side, wump on the other and can't make up your mind what to do.' That was us. We weren't folk, we weren't rock, and we were a whole year too early for folk rock to even exist."

Comedian Bill Cosby was also a client of Roy Silver's, and Denny and my mom spent a lot of time watching Cosby perform. Influenced by his stage act, she and Denny developed a way of talking they dubbed "speaking mugwump," and it became their secret language. "We liked it so much we just used it all the time," Denny recalled. "For instance, if you were to say: 'The swift brown fox jumped over the lazy dog,' in mugwump it would be 'Da quiff browm foph junft ober dat stufid dov.'"

Roy Silver couldn't decide what the new group's next step should be. He brought the four of them back to see his sometime business partner Bob Cavallo at the Shadows in Washington, DC. This time, Cavallo was interested. He agreed to hire them as the house band for the summer of 1964.

Before the band left New York, Denny came to see my mom at her Gramercy Park apartment. She took his hand, grabbed a bottle of LSD, and brought him up onto the roof. My mother must have been enchanted by the prospect of a night together with an expansive view of the city at night and hoped Denny would be too. Romance was on her mind. Denny, however, didn't feel the same way. They sat on the roof of her building that night, took the acid, and listened to her portable record player, the long cord snaking its way back down underneath the staircase door and down to a plug in one of the building's walls.

They talked far into the night. My mom told Denny about the things that she really wanted in life, the things she dreamed about: the picket fence, the Cape Cod-style house on the East Coast, the children someday. Denny later admitted to me that he was too dense to get the hints she was dropping, or maybe he just wasn't paying close enough attention, but my mom wore her heart on her sleeve that night, as she always did. Instead, when she talked about the life she wanted, he thought about the *things* he wanted: the fast cars and all the trappings of material success.

My mom had by then fallen into the uncomfortable pattern of becoming enamored by men who didn't feel the same way about her, a pattern that would repeat itself throughout her life. She never got to experience a relationship of mutuality, one in which each person feels equally as crazy about the other. The men who were in her life on a romantic basis were not only few and far between, but they were also usually there for the rock and roll lifestyle, the good times and the endless parties, not because they loved her passionately. Most nights after performing with the group, after hearing the applause and the audience's cries of "Cass! I love you!," she would return to her hotel room by herself. It must have been such a lonely existence for her.

However, she seemed to have been able to compartmentalize those feelings for Denny and other men and move forward. Maybe she fantasized that being a good friend would be enough to show off her absolute coolness. She was mostly right. As it turned out, my mom's desire to have someone in her life who wasn't going to up and leave her was what led to her desire for a child. It's how I came to be.

When the Mugwumps moved down to Washington for the summer, Roy rented my mom an apartment in Alexandria, Virginia. This meant my mom was close to her family again. It also meant she had space to host friends. She called John Sebastian and invited him down to DC for a few weeks to hang out with her and the new Big 3 at their place, which was worlds beyond any place they'd ever lived in before.

"They were sitting there drinking gin and tonics, and we were struggling it out in New York," Sebastian laughs. "The contrast was notable."

The Mugwumps spent that summer playing shows at the Shadows, with Sebastian on harmonica and Art Stokes, a new addition, on the drums. As Sebastian recalls, the Shadows was an upscale club, with an audience of mostly diplomats and government employees. Among the people who came to see them perform that summer was a young Bill Clinton, who was in law school in Georgetown.

Earlier that summer, Silver and Covallo had ended their business relationship and divided up the talent they mutually represented. Silver took Bill Cosby and a few others, while the Mugwumps stayed on in Cavallo's care. As the summer of 1964 drew to an end, Cavallo realized that to keep the group's momentum going, they would need to head back to New York. He was confident he could get them a contract to make an album.

With that goal in mind, he secured them a booking at the Peppermint Lounge, a wildly popular gay bar in Times Square. Just a few years earlier, the Peppermint Lounge had been the epicenter of the twist craze that quickly spanned the globe, and the club became a favorite dance spot for celebrities ranging from Audrey Hepburn and Judy Garland to Noel Coward and Norman Mailer. The club could hold only 178 people at a time but had already become a coveted gig for aspiring bands of the early 1960s. Artists such as the Beach Boys, the Isley Brothers, and the Four Seasons all played there. For the Mugwumps, this booking was a seriously big deal.

So, the group headed back to New York . . . only to discover that the promise of a big gig at a famous venue came with some unexpected conditions.

First, the accommodations provided for them at the Albert Hotel were far less than fabulous, unless perhaps you were a cockroach. The place had been built as an apartment house in the late 1800s and probably hadn't seen a renovation in almost that long.

Second, by 1964, the Peppermint Lounge was catering to a largely upscale crowd that had been newly turned on to rock and roll. Its customers weren't accustomed to young people with long hair singing folk music. As John Sebastian recalled to me on the phone from his home in Woodstock, New York, "You have to describe the fucking scariness of knowing you're going to follow *Joey Dee*. Joey Dee and the Starliters were the "Peppermint Twist." And the "Peppermint Twist" was one of the biggest records in 1961. Then up comes the Mugwumps and their kind of folk rock. The audience turned their backs, according to Cass."

American folk music had reached the end of its golden era. The Mugwumps would play just that one night at the Peppermint Lounge. As a folk group, they now found themselves behind the times.

CHAPTER 4

THE MUGWUMPS HAD ARRIVED AT A TIPPING POINT. They would have to change their sound if they wanted to continue as a band.

Through the Greenwich Village folk-music grapevine, they heard that a group called the New Journeymen was looking for a singer. The Journeymen had been on the southern leg of the Hootenanny Tour that past winter, the same leg that Denny's Halifax Three had performed on. At that time, as mentioned before, the New Journeymen was composed of its leader, the towering six-foot-five John Phillips, a songwriter and guitarist who'd grown up in Alexandria, Virginia, like my mom; John's strikingly beautiful young blonde wife, Michelle, a native Californian; and a banjo picker named Marshall Brickman. Brickman had recently left the New Journeymen to pursue a career in writing—he would later become an established Hollywood screenwriter and a lead writer on *The Tonight Show*. In the meantime, he'd left John and Michelle in need of another male singer to round out their group.

As Denny has recalled in his off-Broadway show, "Dream a Little Dream,"

Well, The Journeymen had broken up and John & Michelle were now "The New Journeymen" and looking for a tenor to play a tour . . . so, I get the phone call. 'Hello Dennis. John Phillips, The Journeymen? I need a tenor.' John and his wife, Michelle, were living in an apartment on New York's Lower East Side.

The Mugwumps needed money to pay their bills. Something must be done. So, one night I show up at John and Michelle's with a Beatles album under my arm. I have called for reinforcements. Then there was a knock at the door. Michelle answers and there's Cass. She's got on a pink angora sweater, a little white pleated skirt and matching go-go boots. John looks at her and whispers, "Jesus, what is that?" That's the dynamic that was going to play itself out all through their relationship. . . .

Anyway, Cass comes in, introduces herself and announces that she has brought "pressies." She lays a little paper package on the coffee table and carefully unwraps four sugar cubes. LSD-25.

John and Michelle had never taken LSD before that night, but Mitch, like I said, Mitch is always ready for anything. She goes for a cube but John takes it from her and sniffs it like a Cuban cigar. "I think I'd better try that first, darling.'"

See, John had to be in charge, always in control. He knew how everything fit—how it all worked together, but Cass was a leader too and she'd brought the acid. This was her trip, and she wasn't about to let Mr. Phillips commit any psychedelic faux pas.

So, she pops a cube into Michelle's mouth, takes one herself, drags her aside and before you know it, the two of them are yakking away like the best of friends. So, I drop the last cube, slap the Beatles on the hi-fi and crank it.

John said, "It's too simple! It's three chords, Dennis! It's Guantanamera with a beat." It was beneath him. See, John was a "folk artist" and doing very well at it. So, we sat around smoking pot and arguing. Every once and awhile Cass would yell over: "You get off yet?" And John would reply: "No. This stuff is useless."

Then everything started to *shimmer*. Michelle had this big antique birdcage and I found a flashlight and put it inside, huge shadows wrapping around the walls and we're all in the bird cage together. "Oh wow man, this is too cool man." John slides off the sofa into the bottom of the cage and I got him. So, I put the stereo speakers on either side of his head and play the Beatles one more time.

"Now, write a lot of songs like this!" Denny told John. That, John heard. Loud and clear.

Years later, Denny would learn from Michelle that she and my mom had a conversation that night that went something like this:

CASS: Isn't he groovy, Michelle?

MICHELLE: Oh yeah, Cass, Denny sings great.

CASS: Not the voice, the ass.

MICHELLE: You and Denny?

CASS: Fat girls need love too, Michelle.

MICHELLE: Mumm—now that you mention it, he looks a lot like John Lennon.

At the time, John and Michelle had a little less than a few thousand dollars in their accounts. But they also had a new American Express card in the name of the New Journeymen. John suggested they take a vacation. A big map was hanging on the apartment wall, so they blindfolded Michelle, spun her around a few times, and told her to point to a place. They would go wherever fate decided. Her finger landed on the Virgin Islands. It was the perfect place for a getaway, and three tickets were purchased for John, Michelle, and Denny.

My mom wasn't part of their plan. Denny told me John had other visions for the group, more akin to a Peter, Paul and Mary type trio. Besides not needing a fourth harmony, my mom's physical image wasn't up to John's standards for his group. "Her eyes are too close together," Denny told me he'd said. "Her voice isn't right for the group. She can't hit the notes."

Off to the Virgin Islands the New Journeymen went. Without my mom. For the moment, at least.

A couple of weeks into the trip, Denny was on the beach one afternoon when he saw a figure approaching from the distance, a small speck that became larger and larger as it grew closer. Shielding his eyes from the sun, Denny squinted into the distance trying to discern whom this might be.

"I don't believe my fucking eyes," he exclaimed. "It's Cass!"

My mother had decided to get out of New York City for a while, but I suspect she mostly wanted to hang out with Denny. The beach life couldn't have been bad either, but I have a difficult time imagining my mom camping on sand for an extended period of time. No self-respecting Jewish American princess ever likes roughing it. My mom had also again brought what she referred to as "pressies" for everyone, in the form of a small bottle of liquid LSD. The party had indeed arrived.

John had met a man named Duffy who owned a hotel on Creque's Alley on the island of St. Thomas. Other hotels nearby had begun to have live music at night as entertainment, and John was able to convince Duffy that his group would be able to fit that bill. With some renovations, a de facto club was created quickly.

John, Michelle, and Denny continued to "work" at Duffy's, playing their music as the New Journeymen while my mom waited tables and added the fourth harmony from wherever she was on the floor. Calling it out, if you will. She felt certain John would come around and ask her to join them if she made it so.

The clientele at Duffy's was rude and relentlessly teased my mother, John Phillips would later recall in his 1986 autobiography *Papa John*. Customers would say things like, "Hey, Fatty, you forget my food? What did you do, eat it all yourself?" My mom would just take the shit and do her job, but eventually Denny had heard enough. When an obnoxious guy started up with my mom, this time Denny jumped off the stage and punched the guy right in the nose.

Denny also remembered my mom singing along from the floor, loud enough that you could hear her from the stage. "And she sounds great," he said. And John says: "Oh yeah, she sounds great now, that's because she's got those three extra notes on the top of her range since she got hit on the head that time."

What?

As Denny recalled, during the renovations at Duffy's, somebody threw a coil of copper tubing from the ice machine out the window and into Creque's Alley. My mom was walking by when it came sailing through the air, hit her on top of the head, and knocked her out cold.

It was this concussion that, according to John, added three notes to the top of my mother's vocal range. This story would be repeated ad nauseum for decades to come in television and print interviews, whenever John was asked why he had hesitated to have my mother join the group. He always maintained that—miraculously—following the concussion, my mother's voice changed its register and became higher, allowing for the perfect blend of the four voices to take place.

Really? That's a fun story, but it's not usually how concussions work. Hitting someone on the noggin doesn't make them sing higher; it gives them a brain injury. The real story is that John didn't like my mother's look. She wasn't skinny and pretty like Michelle. But the girl could sing: that much was undeniable. So, he made up the story about a fake increase in vocal range to justify his choice to finally add my mom to the band months later.

Over time even my mother began to repeat the story as fact, telling everyone she'd begun to sing higher after the injury. She'd even chuckle while recalling the farce in interviews. Maybe she was so happy to finally be added to the band after they returned to California that she didn't want to jeopardize her position. Or maybe the fact that John had been reluctant to include her at the beginning, which she knew was because of her appearance, was so embarrassing that she didn't want to bring it up.

As she had learned early on, the best way to deal with an uncomfortable situation is with humor. While she was always known as being happy and outgoing on the outside, on the inside my mom wanted to be thin and conventionally attractive like everyone else. To have been excluded on account of her weight, something she'd tried so hard and been unable to control, must have been excruciatingly painful. I imagine she'd been loath to reexperience that pain on a continual basis. And so it was with humor that she told this story about being invited to join the Mamas and the Papas. To have a funny story to recall may have been the easiest way for her to handle the memory of those early weeks of rejection.

But first the four musicians had to come back to the US. As Denny recalls, my mom left the islands first, thinking that John wouldn't hire her and Denny wouldn't fight for her inclusion in the band. She'd been the only one with the foresight to buy a round-trip ticket, so she headed back to the States.

When John went to the local American Express office to get money to buy flights home to the US, the agent there took one look at the credit card and unceremoniously cut it in half. The card was in arrears and was on the repossession list. Now the New Journeymen were truly broke. This experience later led to the lyric "greasin' on the American Express card" in the Mamas and the Papas' song "Creeque Alley." But even if they'd known that was coming, it would have been little solace to the stranded musicians, who had to find a way back home.

Back visiting her old haunts in Greenwich Village, my mom discovered many of her folk music friends had begun to migrate to the West Coast. Jim Hendricks and his wife, Vanessa, had already made the move, as had her friend Barry McGuire, who'd been with the New Christy Minstrels. David Crosby had also headed back west, where he was originally from, and had formed a new folk rock group called the Byrds. By the summer of 1965, the Byrds' cover of Bob Dylan's "Mr. Tambourine Man" was already on the charts. The music business continued to change, with rock and roll beginning to include what was referred to as surf music. Groups like the Beach Boys and Jan and Dean had started to dominate the hit charts. Record companies had subsequently opened regional offices in cities like Los Angeles.

Finding the Village almost completely deserted by everyone she knew, my mom decided to travel to Los Angeles as well. Rumor has it that she moved into the basement of the Canyon Store in Laurel Canyon. If you go there even today, you'll find posters of her as well as a portable stereo playing the Mamas and the Papas music on a loop most days. The truth is, she never lived in that space. No self-respecting Jewish American princess would live in a basement with no windows. Jim and Vanessa had invited her to stay with them when she arrived, and that's exactly what she did.

It must have felt wonderful to be reunited with her friends, many of whom were now living in Laurel Canyon. A few weeks after she arrived, so did her comrades from the islands, John, Michelle, and Denny. Having nowhere to stay, they also took Jim and Vanessa up on the generous offer to have everyone crash at their place in Laurel Canyon for a while.

Laurel Canyon, tucked in the hills above Sunset Boulevard, was the growing epicenter of the hippie folk scene in LA. Laurel Canyon Boulevard's winding, two-lane road divides the canyon in half, with tiny streets branching off to the right and left. Each small street off the main canyon road contained small houses, many perched precariously on hillsides, some built practically on top of each other. Laurel Canyon, with all of its many artists and musicians, felt as if Greenwich Village had been airlifted out of New York City and transplanted to Southern California.

Sleeping on mattresses strewn across the floors, the New York transplants lived communally at Jim and Vanessa's place. "There's an eviction notice on the front door and the gas had been turned off, but the electricity was still on," Denny remembers. "Hey, a kid from the North End of Halifax? I tore a space heater off the wall and set it up like a hot plate."

John played his twelve-string guitar, Chunga, endlessly. When the three members of the Journeymen rehearsed in the living room, my mother would add her fourth harmony just as she had done when waiting tables back at Duffy's. Perhaps, my mom had just *known* she should be singing with them, that they had something very special and cool happening. Just as she'd paired John Sebastian and Zal Yanovsky back in the Village in 1964, she had an almost mystical prescience about which musicians would sound good together. Her insight was spot on. By the time she arrived in Los Angeles, the Lovin' Spoonful's "Do You Believe in Magic?," their first single, had risen to number nine on the *Billboard* Hot 100.

The foursome was also developing its own sound. Soon my mom made a phone call to her old friend Barry McGuire from

Greenwich Village. Barry was also living in Laurel Canyon and had become well-known in the LA folk-rock scene. His song "The Eve of Destruction," released in August of 1965, was climbing the *Billboard* charts.

Barry came over to Jim and Vanessa's place to hang out. Upon hearing the four voices together (my mom's included), he was simply blown away. He insisted the group come to the studio with him, where he was in the midst of recording new material with a producer named Lou Adler. They were working at the legendary United Western Recorders at 6000 Sunset Boulevard, where artists like Frank Sinatra, Elvis Presley, and the Beach Boys had made the studio into one of the most revered recording spaces in Hollywood. Even though my mom was not yet an official member of the group, they convinced her to join them at the audition. John must have realized her voice completed their sound.

The foursome performed a few of the songs they had rehearsed in the Virgin Islands and perfected in Jim and Vanessa's living room. Lou listened closely as they sang, his eyes closed in concentration, his head nodding in appreciation as he heard the perfect four-part harmonies John Phillips had meticulously arranged.

John would soon become known for his perseverance in attaining vocals as close to perfection as possible, insisting they be done over and over until a certain *sound* was achieved, almost as if a magical state was achieved with the perfect balance and blend of the four voices until a fifth voice—an overtone—was created. For the group, this was the moment that nirvana was attained. They had a name for this overtone: Harvey. It came from the title of a 1950 movie in which James Stewart played Elwood P. Dowd, a man who befriends a spirit who takes the form of a human-sized rabbit that only he can see. That was Harvey.

As Denny remembered in his play:

There we are, Hollywood, California, Western Recorders, Studio Three singing for Lou Adler. We sing him "California Dreamin.'" We sing him "Straight Shooter." We sing him "Monday, Monday." And after every song out of the booth comes: "Ah, you got any more?" Then, Lou comes out of the booth and says: "So, what do you guys want?" And bam, John goes into business mode: "No, no, Lou it's not what we want, man, it's what we need. See, what we need is a steady stream of money from your office to our house, but we don't have a house yet. And even if we had a house, we don't have a car to get there in and if we had a car . . ." "OK, OK, here's five thousand dollars, go find a house and I'll send somebody out to buy a car."

The next day when they all returned to the studio, contracts were strewn about on the floor. Four copies, one for each of the four band members: John, Michelle, Denny, and my mom, at long last part of the official equation.

A record deal so soon after arriving in LA? This was practically unheard of. The four were so excited that without so much as a consultation or negotiation they readily signed the contracts at an extraordinarily low royalty rate of 5 percent of 90 percent of retail prices payable to the group. The group was given an advance of $5,000 against future sales, which they then went and bought a used car with. Because you can't get anywhere in LA without a car. Literally and figuratively. They bought a 1959 Buick convertible they called Harold the Bleak.

Denny admitted later that "the joke was on all of us. We'd just signed the big deal with Dunhill Records. Wonderful company. They took care of recording, publishing, and management, all under one roof. 'Don't worry, kids, these contracts cover everything.' Did they ever. Their attorneys were our attorneys." Anyone see an issue here?

Still living together for the time being, the band members returned home, and my mother prepared her specialty, duck a l'orange. After they indulged in the sumptuous meal, much wine, brandy, and weed were consumed, and the four of them lounged about watching television together. Denny remembered:

We're all just lying around vegging out watching the tube and trying to come up with a name for the group. "The New Journeymen" was not a handle that was going to hang on this outfit. John was pushing for "The Magic Cyrcle." Nobody liked that, but none of us could come up with anything better, and Cass is just flipping through the channels and this talk show comes and the Hells Angels are being and the first thing we hear is: "Now hold on there, Hoss. Some people call our women cheap, but we just call them our Mamas."

Cass jumped up: "Yeah! I want to be a Mama." And Michelle is going: "We're the Mamas! We're the Mamas!"

OK. I look at John. He's looking at me going: "Mama, mamas . . . Papas? The Mamas and the Papas." Problem solved. A toast! To the Mamas and the Papas.

After dinner was eaten, and the band had its new name, my mother and John both passed out from all the celebratory toasts. While the two of them slumbered on drunkenly, Denny and Michelle crept into the vacant apartment next door and consummated the illicit affair that had been simmering below the surface since the days back in the Virgin Islands. Michelle had confessed to her husband then that a bit of flirting had been going on between them on the beach there, and John reassuringly told her not to worry about it, that Denny would *never* fall for her. John caught them nearly red-handed and was understandably pissed. "If there's one thing that you don't do," he told Michelle, "is fuck my TENOR!"—and then he moved in with said tenor as his new roommate, mostly to be able to keep a close eye on him.

John would soon after write the song, "I Saw Her Again Last Night" *with* Denny about Denny's dalliance with his wife. Was this punishment in some way, or perhaps a way for him to process the affair? I'm not sure. John Phillips once referred to writing the song as a way of "turning tragedy into publishing," which in this case he certainly did.

Denny recalled, "The pressure was building up—on a whole bunch of levels. So, one weekend we all pile into Harold the Bleak and off to Mexico—where we throw ourselves into a vat of tequila. I don't remember how or why. . . . All I remember is the Mexican heat. Night. Drunk, top down, Cass and I in the backseat, careening along the coast highway with Cass watching the speedometer and yelling 'Eighty, ninety, a hundred . . .' and then . . . screeching of brakes, slide, full stop. Slewed across the center line." My mom was scrunched over, crying. Denny had told her about Michelle. He told me, "She called me an asshole! She said, 'Stop thinking with your dick. Try thinking with your big head for a change. She likes me better than she likes you. She doesn't really like either one of you. She loves herself more than anybody in the fuckin' world anyway—you both know that. Michelle will never leave John for you . . . ah, take me home, shithead.'"

My mom must have been furious. She had told Michelle how she'd felt about Denny the first night they'd met back in Greenwich Village. Michelle *knew* my mom had a crush on him, and now my mom knew what had happened between them. "You can have anybody you want, and you still took him," she told Michelle. "You knew how I felt."

This was an offense that would not soon be forgotten, to be sure. My mother would be certain of that.

Once the record deal had resulted in some cash flow, my mother moved into an apartment in West Hollywood at the Sunset Towers, a beautiful art deco building built in the 1930s.

The deal had been signed in September of 1965, the band was rushed into the recording studio, and on December 8, 1965, "California Dreamin'" was released by Dunhill Records. It debuted on the charts in January of 1966 and peaked at number four in March of the same year, spending seventeen weeks in the *Billboard* Top 100. The record was certified gold by June of 1966. In just their first year of existence, the Mamas and the Papas were on their way to incredible success and notoriety.

The group performed their first live show as part of the Sonny and Cher Appreciation Concert at the Hollywood Bowl on April 2, 1966. Also on the bill that evening were Jan and Dean, Donovan, Otis Redding, the Turtles, and the Modern Folk Quartet. The Hollywood Bowl was a hell of a place to start off, and as it turned out, it would also be the venue for the band's last official show. Just a little over two years later, on a summer night in August 1967, they performed their final show with Jimi Hendrix as their opening act.

"Monday, Monday," the second single from the first album, was released in June of 1966, and it ascended quickly to the number one position on the *Billboard* Hot 100 charts, shipping

150,000 copies the first week it was released. With Denny's lilting lead vocals taking center stage, the song was a huge hit. What was really just a silly song about a day of the week that most people dread, "Monday, Monday" turned out to be one of the band's most well-known songs. It would be the Mamas and the Papas' only number one song.

The fruits of success soon arrived in the form of royalty checks. Charge accounts were opened at the fanciest of boutiques in Beverly Hills. Expensive cars were purchased. My mother bought an Aston Martin, and John and Michelle bought matching Jaguars. Denny finally got that Cadillac he'd dreamed about on the rooftop back in New York City that night with my mom.

And things were changing within the dynamic of the foursome, too. Interpersonally, that is. Michelle and John would continue to have strife in their marriage but soldier on, separating at times and getting back together. Around this time, they were both dating other people despite being married still. Remember, this was the sixties, and the idea of "free love" was a term well used and subsequently enjoyed by many. John had taken up with a friend of the couple, Ann, and Michelle had been seeing Gene Clark of the Byrds.

On June 4 of that year, the Mamas and the Papas were scheduled to perform at Melodyland, a venue in Anaheim, California, across the street from Disneyland. Melodyland was a 3,200-seat theater in the round. The opening act was Simon and Garfunkel, whose single "The Sounds of Silence" had achieved huge success. They were touring in support of their album and their new single "Homeward Bound." Then it was the Mamas and the Papas' turn. The four singers went to take their respective positions on the stage.

As they began to sing, it was impossible not to notice Gene Clark, a guest of Michelle's, sitting in the very front row. Although both John and Michelle had been exercising freedom in their marriage, seeing Gene right there in the front row caused John to fly off the handle. He stopped the show immediately.

The situation had become so uncomfortable for John that he decided that he couldn't work with Michelle any longer. He came to Denny and my mom a few days later and let them know that either he was out, or Michelle was. It was up to them. The obvious choice was to keep John. He was the brains and talent behind the songs and the intricate vocal arrangements that made their music so incredible. As one of the singers, Michelle was replaceable and as such, not necessary in John's eyes.

The lawyers at the record company agreed, and on June 28, 1966, they drew up an official letter to Michelle. Her services as a Mama were no longer needed, the letter stated, and furthermore she was to refrain from referring to herself as Mama Michelle in the future. All three members signed the letter, which was then delivered to Michelle. I would imagine that my mother must have felt a sense of having had the last word, that perhaps karma had come to visit for a spell. I'm sure she signed that letter with a certain flourish of her pen.

———

Right around this time my mom decided to try to have a baby. She told her friend, folk singer Judy Henske, that she just wanted to have someone in her life who was always going to be there and never leave her. Someone who was her very own. Besides, she was a rock star, an independent woman. She could do it all by herself. She would stop being careful when she had "relations" and see what happened.

With Michelle out of the group, the band had a new problem. The Mamas and the Papas were scheduled to go on a mini tour of the East Coast and were now down a member. As it turned out, Lou Adler was dating a young woman at the time named Jill Gibson, who looked very similar to twenty-two-year-old Michelle. She would do just fine. Before leaving on the tour, the group went into the studio to finish recording their second album, the self-titled *The Mamas and the Papas*. Jill was installed as the new Mama, and new tracks were recorded with Jill singing all of Michelle's parts. New pictures were snapped of her and superimposed over existing photographic artwork. The first single, released in July of 1966, was "I Saw Her Again," the song written about Denny and Michelle's previous affair. How appropriate the timing was, as history just had repeated itself.

Michelle had all but been removed from the equation, and the new foursome departed for New York, where they were booked to perform as part of the Forest Hills Music Festival on August 6, 1966. The festival was held in Queens, at the Forest Hills Tennis Stadium, which held 13,000 people. The band was again on the same bill as Simon and Garfunkel. In addition to the regular foursome, the Mamas and the Papas also included a drummer and a hired left-handed bass player to round out the stage.

The stage was set at ground level along with the audience, and the group performed four songs. They were part way through "Monday, Monday" when the audience began to notice that Mama Michelle was missing, and they'd been duped. Rushing forward to investigate and chanting "Where's Michelle?," the crowd scared the hell out of the band members, who hastily retreated to the waiting limos and back to the Sherry-Netherland Hotel in New York City.

The Sherry-Netherland was—and still is—an upscale hotel on the Upper East Side of Manhattan, across the street from Central Park. My mother had taken a suite there, and she brought the group's handsome left-handed bass player back to her room with her. There was Chinese food, drinking, and extracurricular fun. Apparently, they had quite the party, doing such a large degree of damage to the suite that the band was politely asked to not return again.

After the fiasco in Forest Hills, it became obvious that Mama Jill wasn't fooling anyone. She was no Mama Michelle, who wasn't as replaceable as they had all previously thought. So it was back to Los Angeles, where Michelle was waiting at the airport when they arrived. She and John had since reconciled, and she was eagerly awaiting her husband's return. My mom and Denny walked by first, saying hello to Michelle as they proceeded to their cars and departed. John got into the car with Michelle, and the Mamas and the Papas were reunited.

CHAPTER 5

THE EXTRACURRICULAR ACTIVITY IN NEW YORK City with the bass player resulted in good news for my mom when she visited her doctor in the fall of 1966. She was expecting, and she was thrilled. Going to the studio, she informed the rest of the group of her pregnancy.

John's immediate reaction was, "When are you having the abortion?" He was concerned about the future of his group more than anything else.

"You don't understand," my mom told him. I'm having this baby." And that was that. Even when the band's management "went through the roof," according to Denny, she stuck to her decision. Having a baby as a single mom in 1967 should have been a scandal, but my mom set a new standard. Besides, she and Jim Hendricks were still technically married, so it was his name that was listed on my birth certificate. "The whole world loved Mama Cass," Denny recalled, "and if Mama Cass wanted to have a baby on her own, well, why not?"

Even when pregnant, my mom didn't slow down for one second. The band's star was rising, and so was hers. Their second album, *The Mamas and the Papas*, went top ten. The song "Dedicated to the One I Love" hit number three on the charts. She also continued to record the group's new album— their third in a single year—which was dubbed *Deliver* in tribute to her current state. The album cover for *Deliver* featured the four band members fully clothed, crowded together in the shallow end of the swimming pool at John and Michelle's Bel Air house. They were gathered together with my mom holding onto Denny's shoulder for support. All of their mouths were open to catch water dripping from holes in the black hat John held up in his hands. Of course, since he was the leader of the group, they were posed drinking from *his* hat. Talk about symbolism.

Then it was back to touring. This time, they were going in style, becoming one of the first—if not the first—rock and roll bands to travel by private Lear jet. Not wanting the band to become overexposed, the management had put a cap on the number of shows and cherry-picked which ones the band would do. Traveling by private jet made the tour all the sweeter, I'd imagine.

Remembered Denny:

We're touring—hopping about the Midwest in a private Lear jet, honking on a four-stemmed hookah full of hash. So, it doesn't seem as awful as it is. Our first flight we ask the pilot,

I mean there's no door, he's right there, you know. "What she'll do?" "Well, I'll tell you, son, this here is a piece of Swedish air force equipment. She'll do 670 miles an hour. Oh yeah, let me tell you something—we take this sucker up to 70,000 feet, hit the apex and go over the top, you're weightless."

Cass hears "weightless" and says: "Oh please, sir, let's hit the apex." So, the pilot says, "OK, but I don't want anybody gettin' hurt so go back to your seats and strap yourself in real tight."

"OK, OK, everybody get strapped in, we're going to hit the apex. Strap in. OK, we're strapped in. Hit the apex." So, Roger Ramjet hits the stick and we go up to seventy thousand feet, hit the apex, and as we go over the top, we pop our seatbelts and we are flying. And for the first time in her life Cass didn't weigh a thing.

To not have her body weighing her down for once in her life must have felt magical.

Back in November of 1966, the second single from the album *The Mamas and the Papas*, "Words of Love," had been released. It featured my mom on lead vocal, but there is a little history lesson here. Initially, John had intended for the song to be sung by Michelle, who wasn't feeling it. Turning to my mother, Michelle told her to sing it. My mom didn't really want to do it, and started making excuses as to why she couldn't. Finally, John had heard enough. Knowing my mother's vocal prowess, he pushed her, as he had done time and time again in the past.

He knew what she was capable of even if she didn't, after all this time.

A grand piano sat in the middle of the studio. Handing her a microphone and a chair, John insisted that my mom get up onto the piano's top and cut the vocal. Annoyed, my mom climbed atop the piano. The playback began, and she recorded the lead vocal in one take. When she was done, she dropped the microphone on the piano top, saying sarcastically, "You got that?"

Then she promptly left the studio. Point made.

On November 11, the group performed at New York City's coveted Carnegie Hall. This was the ultimate achievement, and one my mother was thrilled about. During shows, she was known to have a connection with the audience, often regaling them with her humor and her candor. Sitting down on the apron of the stage at Carnegie Hall that night, she heard someone yell from the crowd, "I love you, Cass!" to which she immediately replied, "Dynamite! Where are you staying?"

Exactly one month after Carnegie Hall on December 11, 1966, the Mamas and the Papas appeared on *The Ed Sullivan Show* in New York. This, too, was a pinnacle of success to appear on one of the most popular shows on American television at that time. The band performed three songs on the show: "California Dreamin'," "Monday, Monday," and their new single, "Words of Love." Ed loved them, perpetually flubbing the group's name in classic Ed Sullivan fashion. "The Puppas and the Mummas!" he exclaimed.

Although the album had been mostly recorded in the fall of 1966, *Deliver* was released in February of 1967. Now almost seven months along in her pregnancy, my mom was finally home and off the road. She had worked tirelessly and was ready for a break. By then she had moved out of the Sunset Towers and into a house she'd bought above Laurel Canyon. She'd looked at a number of houses before deciding on a Cape Cod-style home, likely one that reminded her of houses on the East Coast where she'd grown up. I imagine she hoped to fill it with friends and family and surround herself with people, but I doubt she could have had any idea how legendary that house would become.

The Mamas and the Papas were nominated for a Grammy award for Best Vocal Performance by a Group for "Monday, Monday." But my mom was home on that night of March 15, 1967, heavily pregnant, when her bandmates accepted the Grammy award. She was only about six weeks away from giving birth.

The band was nominated along with one of the finest harmony groups at the time: the Beach Boys, who were nominated for their song "Good Vibrations." My mom was friendly with Bruce Johnston of the Beach Boys, and they were amused by the fact that they were nominated against one another in the same category. In those days, when people received nominations for Grammy Awards, they were sent official certificates of their nominations. My mom and Bruce decided it would be great fun to switch nomination certificates and did exactly that.

Six weeks later, on April 26, 1967, I was born at Cedars of Lebanon Hospital in Hollywood. After enduring more than twenty-four hours of labor, my mother underwent a Cesarean section. She named me Owen Vanessa Hendricks, signing my birth certificate as Cass Hendricks. She was, after all, still married on paper. Now she had her Owen, her very own. She spent a week in the hospital, and when we came home, a hired nurse helped her with recovery and infant care.

The Summer of Love was just beginning. Plans for the Monterey Pop Festival had already been hatched.

The lineup at the Monterey Pop Festival would go down in history as legendary: the Grateful Dead, Jefferson Airplane, Jimi Hendrix, Janis Joplin, Otis Redding, Ravi Shankar, Simon and Garfunkel, and the Who. John wrote one of his best songs and gave it to his childhood friend, Scott McKenzie, to sing. It was one of the longest titles in pop music history, a song called "If You're Going to San Francisco (Be Sure to Wear Some Flowers in Your Hair)." It went straight up the charts and thousands of "flower children" started heading west.

In June of 1967, my mom traveled north from Los Angeles to the festival in Monterey with six-week-old me and a baby nurse in tow. Her sister, Leah, also came along, having moved to California to pursue her own dream of becoming a singer and songwriter. The Mamas and the Papas were scheduled to close out the two-day music festival, following a long list of powerhouse musicians. When Janis Joplin took the stage and began to sing, my mother was sitting in the audience, next to Leah, with her mouth agape, mouthing the words, "Oh, wow."

On the final day, following a particularly raucous set by the Who, the Mamas and the Papas took the stage. The Who had, as usual, destroyed the amplifiers on stage at the end of their set, and the sound was now predictably terrible.

"Someone asked me the other day, when am I going to have the baby?" my mom quipped to the crowd from the stage. "That's funny . . ." she trailed off. Yet again, she felt the impulse to turn a rude comment into something humorous to make it tolerable.

Denny had arrived literally minutes before showtime. He'd been on an island drinking himself into a stupor for a few weeks until that very day, but managed to get to Monterey just in time to perform. So much was off kilter that day, and as the four of them stood together on the stage, something just didn't feel the same anymore. So much water had flowed under the bridge by then, and so many feelings had been hurt along the way. The relationship dramas within the group had caused irreparable rifts, and the damage done was the loss of the familial connection the foursome had once shared. Where they'd once been four people barely making ends meet and trying to find a break together, now they were each rich and famous beyond their wildest imaginations. The thirst to create something new and exciting together had been quenched, and now they were four individual people starting to live four separate lives.

Back in Los Angeles, John and Michelle had taken the plunge into real estate with the purchase of a beautiful Tudor-style mansion on Bel Air Road that had previously belonged to Hollywood actress Jeanette MacDonald. They embarked on an extensive remodel of the house complete with a home recording studio built in the existing attic space and a cedar-lined, walk-in closet. Building his own recording studio would cut down on recording costs. It meant no additional time would be needed for traveling between his house and the studio; everything that was needed would be under one roof. One could ostensibly just roll out of bed and into the studio no matter what time of day or night. Food, drink, and questionable substances would be available on demand.

It also meant there were no limits on the number of hours or time of day that anyone could work, and the sessions frequently became extensively long and tedious. Two years later my mother remarked to *Rolling Stone* that recording just the vocals for one song in John's studio could take a whole month, while her entire debut solo album required only ten days in a studio, singing live with a band.

The Mamas and the Papas soon began recording their fourth studio album. The entire album was recorded at John and Michelle's studio in Bel Air. Recording at home allowed for a more casual schedule, and the process was slow. Among the most notable of songs on the album, and the last single released, was a remake of a song called "Dream a Little Dream of Me," which had first been recorded in 1931 by Ozzie Nelson. It would later be released by many other notable artists, including Doris Day, and later as a duet by Ella Fitzgerald and Louis Armstrong.

On occasion, the Mamas and the Papas would use this song as a warm-up, and it was familiar to them. According to John, he'd had to convince my mom to sing it for the album. She thought it was corny, and he had to talk her into whistling and singing the *bah-da-dahs* at the end. It was his vision, and she sang it like a champ.

Between the sessions, appearances and concerts had also been scheduled, so the group reluctantly headed out again to do a few shows a month. But they were starting to wind down energetically, artistically, and otherwise. On August 18, 1967, they performed what would be their final show as a group at the Hollywood Bowl, with Jimi Hendrix as their opening act.

By then, it was clear to all of them that Harvey had left the building, and the group was barely holding it together. Recording ground to a halt. In mid-September of 1967, John called a press conference to announce that the group was taking some time off to regroup and reevaluate. They wouldn't be releasing any new material for a while. But first, the Mamas and the Papas had been booked for another appearance on the

Ed Sullivan Show, where Ed asked them about the rumors that they were breaking up.

"It's not true," my mom insisted. "We're not leaving the business."

"Well, the report we got back here was that you were splitting up, I didn't want to take it up with you. . . ." Ed began before my mother interrupted him to say, "No, you can take it up with us because it's not true, we're just going away."

The audience clapped loudly, and she continued, "Have faith! We're just going away on a vacation. An adventure. Seeking treasure. . . ."

"Where are you going?" Ed asked.

"We don't really know," John answered. "We're leaving on *The France* on Thursday, from here. I'm not sure where it lands," he chuckled. "It goes to France, I think," Michelle added with dubious authority, having a true blonde moment.

The ship was actually bound for England so the band could perform at Albert Hall in London as one of their final booked engagements. But before beginning the journey across the ocean, the ship made a stop in Boston to pick up more passengers. The group disembarked and immediately procured half a pound of marijuana for the crossing to be enjoyed by everyone. The days on board were filled with good food, drinks, and the smoking of the aforementioned Boston pot until just before docking, when John and Michelle were approached by the ship's purser. He informed them that the constable was waiting for my mother on the dock in Southampton. That was the extent of the information they received.

My mom and Michelle had spent the last day on the boat sewing what pot was left into the linings of their coats in order to smuggle it off the boat. Now that was out of the question, and my mom, in a panic, set about trying to flush all of the remaining marijuana down the ship's toilet. She didn't know why she was about to be arrested, but she did know that if marijuana was also found, she would be in even more trouble.

Michelle recalled going into the bathroom to help. "Cass was crying," she wrote in her 1987 memoir *California Dreamin'*. "There was marijuana from one end of the bathroom to another. She was scooping it all up and trying to flush it down the toilet, and it wouldn't flush away; every time she pulled the handle the pot just remained, floating on top of the water. And it was just everywhere, in the room and on her clothing and all over her hands. It was such a mess and looked so silly."

"I think you should go back to John," my mom said. "I'll take care of this."

Upon docking in Southampton, my mother was promptly arrested and taken to Scotland Yard, allegedly due to an unpaid hotel bill and blankets and towels that had been absconded with on her previous trip to England. Not by her, to be clear, but by a male companion who'd been staying with her and had departed after she had left the hotel. Nevertheless, she was the responsible party and was held overnight at Scotland Yard. The concert was subsequently canceled. When she was brought to court the following day, she was released relatively quickly, and a warrant was issued for the boyfriend who had been the hotel linen thief. She left without a stain on her character, as the magistrate decreed upon her release. My mom remarked to the press that the policemen were wonderful, but that she didn't think much of the jails. Ironically, there hadn't been enough blankets. She'd been cold. "Believe me," she said, "One blanket doesn't go far around this chick."

To celebrate her release, a party was thrown that night. Among the guests were some newer English friends, the members of the Rolling Stones. Recalling the entire ordeal to her new friend Mick Jagger, my mother told the tale of her jailhouse experience in full drama and color before John interrupted her to say she was relating the story incorrectly. My mother became infuriated and mortified that John had embarrassed her in front of Mick Jagger. She'd been the one arrested and put into jail; it was her story to tell. How dare he correct her? Denny said that she came pounding on his hotel room door later that night, yelling that she'd finally had it.

She was done with the Mamas and the Papas.

Although the group was technically on a break and not recording any new music, there was still material from the new album that had been recorded at John and Michelle's home studio and was ready to be released. Dunhill put out the band's fourth album, titled *The Papas and the Mamas*, in June of 1968. The first single, "Safe in My Garden," failed to break into the Top

40. Perhaps realizing that the magic of the group was fading, Dunhill released the second single, "Dream a Little Dream of Me" featuring my mom on the solo vocal. They marketed it as "Mama Cass with the Mamas and the Papas" in America and simply as "by Mama Cass" in the UK.

"Dream" was the final single released by the Mamas and the Papas. It peaked in August of 1968 on the *Billboard* Hot 100 at number twelve, reached number eleven on the equivalent British charts, and spent two weeks in the number one position on the Australian charts. Despite her initial misgivings about recording it, to this day, "Dream" remains one of the songs for which my mom is best known and also one of the most successful songs released by the group.

CHAPTER 6

THE MAMAS AND THE PAPAS TAKING A BREAK MEANT that my mom was finally free to proceed as a solo artist and record music of her choice. However, one of the renegotiations of the recording contracts had included what's known as "a first right of refusal" clause, which meant that if any member of the Mamas and the Papas were to strike out on their own, the record company (Dunhill in this case) would have the right to make the first offer to release the new album or turn it down. This gave Dunhill the opportunity to keep my mom on the label as a solo artist, which—having just experienced what could have been described as a Mama Cass hit with "Dream a Little Dream"—they very much wanted to do.

Though the Mamas and the Papas weren't working together, my mom stayed in close touch with Denny. He'd been drinking heavily, spending irresponsibly, and surrounding himself with questionable people. One night, she showed up at his place unannounced.

She said, "Dennis, get your head out of your ass."

"What?" he responded.

"You're going to get screwed, man. You're gonna lose your house. You'll lose everything."

Denny said, "I'd hit bottom, and I didn't really care anymore. But Cass cared. She looked at my old hangdog face and said: 'Aw, Denny, marry me? I can make you happy.'"

"Cass had never verbalized how she felt about me until that night," he continued, "but I knew from the islands, no, from before then, from New York—up on her roof in Gramercy Park. A blizzard. Her big old white portable record player sitting there in the snow playing the theme from *Peyton Place*. The theme from *Peyton Place*? That was 'our song.' I knew she loved me, and I loved her too, but not like she wanted me to. She did weigh three hundred pounds and I wasn't man enough to deal with that. I . . . made some stupid joke. She left and something was lost forever."

That summer, my mom recorded her first solo record at Wally Heider Studios on Cahuenga Boulevard in Hollywood. With producer John Simon, who had recently produced artists like Big Brother and the Holding Company, and the Band, she chose the material for the album. Mostly, she handpicked songs that friends of hers had written, including one by Simon himself called "Talking to My Toothbrush." Also on the album were songs by John Sebastian; "The Room Nobody Lives In," which was later recorded by Elvis Costello; and a Leonard

Cohen song called "You Know Who I Am." So many of her friends' songs were included that she'd initially wanted to call the record *In the Words of My Friends*.

The recording sessions for her debut solo album reportedly took just two weeks, with my mom doing the lead vocals in complete single takes rather than in the repetitive, perfectionistic method that had been the norm in the Phillips' studio. This was a whole new experience, and hers alone. "Alone" being the operative word.

Because "Dream a Little Dream" had been such a big hit, my mother included it on the new record, too. Some sweetening was added to the song to distinguish it from the original. This new version starts with the sounds of a rainstorm, then a radio being tuned into a station that begins playing the introductory notes of "Dream." At the end of another song, titled "California Earthquake," the sounds of sirens and chaos echo in an ominous way. Very psychedelic, and certainly timely for 1968.

The record also featured my mother singing in a lower register than she had in the Mamas and the Papas, adding a more mellow sound to her voice. In the group, she'd been pushed to sing higher notes that were only achieved with a certain amount of force. It can also be quite tiring to the vocal cords.

The cover photograph for my mom's first solo record, *Mama Cass: Dream a Little Dream*, was snapped at our house on Woodrow Wilson Drive on a bright summer day in 1968. Seated on a green Norton-Villiers motorcycle behind her coveted rosebushes, she was casually dressed in a pair of knee-high red suede boots and a long-sleeved purple shirt. She was thinner than she'd been before, having recently lost a tremendous amount of weight. I'm sitting in front of her, barefoot and with my blonde baby hair askew.

After I was born, my mom went on an insane diet, wanting to once and for all lose the weight she'd struggled with all her life. She'd been on many diets in the past, but this one was a real doozy. She fasted five days a week, drinking only water and an occasional glass of orange juice, and then feasted on weekends with steak and green vegetables for the single meal a day she allowed herself. Keeping her intake to under 1,000 calories a day, she dropped 110 pounds—seventy pounds of it in just five months. She lost an incredible amount of weight, but this definitely wasn't the healthiest way to go about it. She was photographed in a slinky long beaded dress standing next to my baby cradle in an article for the *Ladies' Home Journal* in 1968—the kind of image she hadn't been able to project before.

When her first solo record was released in October of 1968, my mother was one of the first women to be featured in the new rock and roll magazine *Rolling Stone*, which had launched less than a year before. She was an hour late for her interview with journalist Jerry Hopkins, coming to him straight from the Dunhill Records offices where she'd heard the playback of her album for the first time. Hopkins asked if she was pleased with it.

"Well, David Crosby said about a dozen times that it took him farther than he'd meant to go, which I thought was such a groovy compliment," she told him. "It's me. It's where I'm at. Some friends came in—Graham Nash of the Hollies, John Sebastian—and they said, 'I'm gonna have to tell you, if it's bad, I'm going to have to tell you, because I really love you and I wouldn't want you to put something out that you're gonna be ashamed of.' I said, 'If it's not great, it's because I'm not great then. Whatever it is, it's where I'm at right now.'"

Also included on her first record was a song called "What Was I Thinking Of?" written by my aunt Leah, who had moved to LA after graduating from high school. Having one of her songs appear on her famous older sister's first solo record was quite an accomplishment for the young songwriter. Leah remembers my mom as her biggest supporter, someone who did all she could to help further her younger sister's budding career. They were proud of each other; that was always clear.

Not long after moving to Los Angeles, Leah fell in love with a fellow musician, a studio drummer named Russell Kunkel. They met at my mom's house in Laurel Canyon through friends and were married in the garden in the backyard in November 1968.

It was around this time that my mother's soon-to-be-legendary, open house, come-on-over-and-hang-out policies were becoming more frequent, even in her absence while she was working or recording. Her open-door policy meant that on any given day, a wide variety of musicians could be found jamming in the backyard under the birch trees or splayed across the living room couches.

"Music happens in my house and that pleases me," my mom told *Rolling Stone*. "If you come over to my house, and you see Eric Clapton and David Crosby and Steve Stills playing guitar together and Buddy Miles walks in, it's not because I got out my Local 47 book and called up and said let's get a bunch of musicians together." (Local 47 was the LA branch of the musicians' union, the American Federation of Musicians).

"My house is a very free house," she continued. "It's not a crash pad and people don't come without calling. But on an afternoon, especially on weekends, I always get a lot of delicatessen food in, because I know David [Crosby] is going to come over for a swim and things are going to happen. Joni Mitchell has written many songs sitting in my living room. Christmas day when we were all having dinner, she was writing songs."

As David Crosby recalled to Eddi Fiegel in *Dream a Little Dream of Me*:

That was a fascinating house, and I spent a great deal of time there. She had probably the nicest house of any of us and there was plenty of room and she was a person that liked having people come over because she was lonesome.

Cass was very sociable and easy to meet and to talk to and funny, so people took to her. Some of the rest of us were a little odder and a little harder to get to know, so she was accessible, and she was a person that people coming over from England into the California scene would key on and then from her, they would make other acquaintances. I know anybody that was visiting in town that I knew, if they were interesting, I would always take them up to Cass's. We would hang out, smoke a joint, laugh, talk, dish other people, all the standard stuff, and with her, it was fun. We'd go over there and mooch food, mooch drugs, hang out, play, say, "What do you think of this?" And we'd sing her something.

An impromptu backyard picnic my mom held in 1968 would be commemorated on film by her good friend, photographer Henry Diltz. She had invited friends over to meet Eric Clapton, who was in town with the band Cream and didn't yet know anyone in the Laurel Canyon scene. She'd met him on a television show and invited him up to the house the next day for a barbecue. In one iconic photograph, Joni Mitchell, David Crosby, and Eric Clapton are sitting on the grass under the birch trees while Joni plays guitar and six-month-old me sits in the forefront, chewing on one of Henry's film canisters. In another photo from that picnic, Eric, Joni, and David sit on a low brick wall balancing paper plates of food on their laps while my mother sits facing them on the grass, holding me in her lap. Micky Dolenz from the Monkees was also there with his new Super 8 camera, capturing everything he found edgy on film. Later, when people would ask him for footage of that day, he'd have endless frames of cigarettes burning in an ashtray.

My mom, with her natural warmth and generous spirit that drew people into her orbit, was at the very nexus of it all. As John Sebastian would later recall, "She held court not in a big office, but in a swimming pool the temperature of pee."

It was at one of these many get-togethers that happened at our house that my mom introduced her friends David Crosby and Stephen Stills—who were "kind of a duo at that moment" as Sebastian describes them—to her friend Graham Nash, who was a member of the Hollies. My mom was incredibly in tune with what Stephen and David were beginning to create and knew that a third voice should be added to their sound. She discussed this with John Sebastian in a conversation he would recall in 2022, at the ceremony dedicating her star on the Hollywood Walk of Fame.

"In the conversation, I may have suggested, 'Oh, what about?' And she said, 'Who do we get to sing above Crosby?' You had to be able to know about vocal ranges and things to be able to make such a comment," he said. "And I was going, 'Well, Phil Everly doesn't like his brother this year. . . .' But Cass had the answer."

One night, right about then, she and Stephen Stills were both watching a show at The Troubadour on Santa Monica Boulevard, in Hollywood. As Stills remembers the encounter, he was standing on the sidewalk after the show. As she came out with the rest of the crowd she walked over and asked how he was doing.

"Oh, I'm great," Stills told her. "David and I are working on songs."

"So do you think you'd like to have a high voice to sing above you two?" she asked.

It would have to be the right kind of guy, Stills told her, because a musical trio often turns into "a marriage that turns into a pressure cooker that turns into a psychotic machine," as he describes it today.

"Well," my mom said, "When David Crosby calls you tomorrow and says come to my house, do it. And don't tell anybody."

Knowing what an "adept queen" she was, Stills says, he got Crosby's call and showed up at our house the next day. "And there was David, and [behind him] in his little lovely Edwardian green vest was Graham Nash, our future. And the rest, as I say, is history. She was the one who envisioned what we would sound like, because she had that much expertise and experience."

Graham Nash has also said there's no doubt in his mind that the sound Crosby, Stills & Nash created was first imagined by my mom, who instinctively knew what her three friends were capable of creating—so much so that hers was the only other voice to appear on their first album. Emotionally, she became a sort of den mother to the group, someone to whom Crosby remembers turning to for love and good advice if he was feeling troubled or depressed.

Once again, my mom had played the role of Great Connector, the Puppeteer of Musical Bands. "She did this all without ever being a record company exec or a publishing mogul," Sebastian explains, with a perfect mix of incredulity and affection. "She did it all with gentle persuasion, touches of *biting* sarcasm, and pure, snuggly, Jewish love."

But having a free, open-to-everyone house also meant that my mother's generosity was frequently taken advantage of. There were hangers-on of all types, many of whom were ingesting a variety of questionable substances. Leah remembers that things could get a little bit nutty at the house, and that people who my mom would never be associated with had she been paying closer attention would gather there. People who'd bring and do drugs and hang out for hours and hours, generally making themselves at home in *our* home.

In an almost parallel universe to this chaotic scene on the ground floor, I was being cared for upstairs by a revolving door of nannies who protected me from the mayhem going on below. These nannies never stayed for very long. I never understood why. As a child, I would become attached to a caregiver and almost as soon as we established a relationship, they would be gone.

Nearly twenty years later, when I returned to live in LA, I reconnected with Naomi Orr, one of the women who'd cared for me after the baby nurse my mom had hired upon my birth departed when I was about six weeks old. Naomi stayed with us until I was eight months old. She had felt a strong connection to me and my mom and had managed to stay in touch with Grandma Bess and called her from time to time. When I asked Naomi why she'd left the job, her answer was twofold: first, that I had reached a point in my development where I had become extremely attached to her, and that there had been more than one occasion that I'd fussed greatly when handed to my mom. Recognizing that she needed to spend more time with me, my mom had let Naomi go reluctantly. Second, as Naomi later confided to me, she'd been constantly concerned that one of the downstairs offenders would attempt to slip something nefarious into my bottle. "It was a crazy time," she recalled.

One of the people who frequented our house at this time was a guy named Pic Dawson. Pic was an extremely bad dude who wiggled his way into my mother's inner circle and eventually became her sometimes boyfriend. He was the one who had absconded with the towels in London and skipped out on the hotel bill, causing my mother to spend the night in Scotland Yard. Pic was the son of a US diplomat and had been sent to private schools where he was groomed to be involved in government, but he turned out to be the black sheep of his family instead. He was heavily involved in using and selling hard drugs and was immediately disliked by almost every one of my mother's friends. He brought a bunch of similar-minded people to the house, and they brought all of their drugs, too.

Concerned for her sister's well-being—as she should have been—and noting that my mom had been appearing out of it lately, Leah did a fast assessment and realized where the drugs were coming from: Pic Dawson.

Leah was twenty years old, only two years out of high school, but she was a badass Cohen woman and knew how to take charge. *No more*, she decided. She told Pic he needed to get the people out of the house, along with *all* of the drugs, and if she found out it wasn't happening, she was going to call the cops. Calling the cops at that point in time was akin to calling in the DEA or the FBI. It wasn't something people liked to have threatened. A big argument ensued, with Pic threatening to harm Leah before he departed.

Meanwhile, the lavish lifestyle my mom had become accustomed to was becoming increasingly costly to maintain. The first and only single from her debut album, "California Earthquake," hadn't done very well. The royalty checks from the Mamas and the Papas were dwindling, and now there was a house to run and a child to support. Not to mention her growing appreciation for the finer things in life. The Limoges china purchased from Neiman Marcus. The elaborate silver pattern and crystal glasses. The sable coat. The Cartier and Tiffany jewelry. She had to find a way to make some money.

Bobby Roberts, who had managed the Mamas and the Papas, managed to get my mother booked for a three-week engagement at Caesars Palace in Las Vegas for a fee of $40,000 a week. That was a huge amount in 1968, the equivalent of more than $300,000 per week today. As she would tell Jerry Hopkins in the *Rolling Stone* interview, "I believe that if you truly dig what you're doing, if you lay it out that way, nobody cannot respond. I think my plans are to just build up, not relent for a moment. That's what rock and roll is. Rock and roll is relentless. That's what I want to do in Vegas—not let up. Really pour it on. Have a band. Bring music and entertainment and relaxation and highness and everything else to Vegas. I don't think it's ever been done there," she said.

On opening night, she was a nervous wreck. A group of her closest friends had come in to support her: Peter Lawford, Jimi Hendrix, Sammy Davis Jr., John and Michelle Phillips. Floral arrangements filled her dressing room from friends who couldn't come to the opening shows. Stepping out on stage put her in her element, but she'd spiked a fever earlier that day and her throat was uncooperative. Not a single note emerged that was in the *neighborhood* of being in tune. She struggled through the set, and before it was over the crowd had begun to shuffle out in disappointment.

A second show was scheduled for that evening, and she somehow made it through. Barely. Again, some of the audience members walked out before the end. She was seriously ill and needed medical attention.

Reviews of opening night were as harsh as one might expect, and the remaining shows were canceled. My mother returned to Los Angeles where she was briefly hospitalized with anemia, tonsillitis, and hemorrhaging vocal cords. She was exhausted and needed to take time to rest and recover.

After recovering from this episode, my mom went back into the studio in Los Angeles in February of 1969. Dunhill had dutifully released her first album without much success, the one she'd had creative control over. Now they stepped in more forcefully in the creation of the second record, titled *Bubblegum, Lemonade & . . . Something for Mama*. Producer and songwriter Steve Barri was installed at the helm. The cover of the album was a beautiful picture snapped by Henry Diltz, who had also taken the cover photograph for her first record. On the cover of *Bubblegum*, Henry and his partner, designer Gary Burden, conceptualized a different sort of design. My mom was dressed in a white dress with white heeled boots, positioned in a white wicker rocking chair with her legs crossed and smiling. Framing her picture is an intricate pink border made from chewed-up bubblegum, which had been provided by Leah, Russ, and other friends who had stopped by that day.

My mother later commented, "Bubblegum music is very pleasant to listen to and maybe that's what I'm supposed to be doing. But it's like they say about Chinese food: Half an hour after tasting it, you're hungry again. Musically it's not quite what I want to be doing. It's a good recording for what it is. But it's not what you'd call social commentary."

That June, *Esquire* magazine ran a feature titled "Sink Along with Mama Cass." It told the story of the Vegas debacle, complete with a description of my mother in her current surroundings. The article depicted her reclining and resting in her humongous, custom-made bed, with a television and small refrigerator in the room, her newly acquired sable coat next to her. The sable would have to be sold, she would tell the journalist sadly, to cover some bills. She was devastated by this, since she'd always dreamed of having one. Burying her bare feet in the sable pelts, she sniffled slightly.

She loved her things, her jewelry, the fine china, the silver, and the crystal glasses she had on display in her dining room. Her business managers, who took care of paying her bills, were constantly telling her to cut back. They'd been known to take her credit cards away to curb her spending. This was not a problem to my mom, who would saunter into the exclusive stores in Beverly Hills, where she would be recognized on the spot. A store charge account would be opened for her, and *voilá*: the new Limoges would be delivered to our house the very next day. Her business manager wouldn't know about her purchases until the bill arrived at the end of the month. I have to admire her perseverance and her propensity for getting the things she wanted.

But now the baubles on hold at Tiffany & Co. would have to be canceled as well, as would the custom Cartier watch. Easy come, easy go.

The first single from the new album, "Move in a Little Closer, Baby," was released in March of 1969 and was a minor hit, followed in May by the lyrically positive "It's Getting Better," written by Barry Mann and Cynthia Weil. Mann and Weil were established songwriters from the famous Brill Building in New York. The Brill Building was the epicenter of music in New York City and was nearly synonymous with hit songs. Countless songwriters wrote some of their most successful hits there. It's where Carole King and Gerry Goffin came up with "Will You Love Me Tomorrow."

On the B side of "It's Getting Better" was a song penned by Leah called "Who's to Blame?," continuing my mom's efforts to promote her sister's songs alongside her own career. "It's Getting Better" peaked at number thirty on the *Billboard* Hot 100 charts, and also at number thirteen on the *Billboard* AC (Adult Contemporary) chart. And in October of 1969, "Make Your Own Kind of Music" was released, also a Mann and Weil composition. On the B side appeared a song called "Lady Love" written by my mom's friend Delaney Bramlett. Delaney had written the song specifically for my mom to sing about her relationship with me. As the music starts my mom says, "I'd like to dedicate this song especially to my little daughter," and begins to sing the campy tune.

"Make Your Own Kind of Music" would reach number thirty-six on the *Billboard* Hot 100 charts and peak at number six on the *Billboard* AC chart. The song had an almost emblematic theme in encouraging people to not only accept themselves as unique individuals, but to do so no matter what anyone else thought or said to them. "Even if no one else sings along," the lyrics say. This song was one of the first that I heard on the radio and recognized as my mom's, realizing it was her voice coming over the airwaves. Over the years, I have been told many times by fans of my mom's that "Make Your Own Kind of Music" helped them find the strength to struggle through adversities.

Knowing that her songs continue to be a source of comfort and inspiration, decades after she left us, would unquestionably make my mom happy. She'd have been grateful to know she made a difference in this world. I can't help reflecting back on my great-grandmother Chaya, who made her way to America to earn her fortune so that she could return to Poland to marry that boy. And only two generations later, her granddaughter became an internationally known rock and roll star. In my very humble opinion, that's the American dream personified.

CHAPTER 7

AS I GREW FROM BABY TO TODDLER TO LITTLE GIRL, my mother found herself wanting to stay close to home to spend as much time with me as possible. That meant finding work in LA, and so she began doing television, soon becoming a frequent fixture on network TV.

The late 1960s was the peak era for television variety shows. In 1969, Andy Williams, Lawrence Welk, Ed Sullivan, Red Skelton, Dean Martin, Leslie Uggams, and Carol Burnett all headlined their own weekly shows, and *Hee Haw* and *Laugh-In* had loyal followings. Because she'd been a guest on so many of these shows, hosting her own show was a natural next step for my mom to take.

Produced by Chuck Barris, *The Mama Cass Television Program* was shot as a pilot for a possible weekly show. The one-hour variety show aired on ABC on June 26, 1969. My mom was paired with actors Martin Landau and Barbara Bain and comedian Buddy Hackett. Most notable was the introduction of one of her new friends, the young Canadian singer-songwriter named Joni Mitchell who had been at her picnic the prior year, now making her first American television appearance. Joni performed her recent single "Both Sides Now" and also sang alongside my mom and Mary Travers of Peter, Paul and Mary in a standout rendition of Bob Dylan's "I Shall Be Released." The way the three women harmonize together is breathtaking. But the powers-that-be at ABC decided not to pick up the option to turn the special into a series. So, my mom had to turn her sights elsewhere for the moment.

From January to September 1970, she appeared as co-host alongside Sam Riddle on the Dick Clark-produced music variety show *Get It Together* that aired every Saturday night on ABC. She was also a series regular on *The Ray Stevens Show* over the summer that year. And she was a cast favorite on *The Carol Burnett Show*, according to Carol, who I was lucky enough to speak with by telephone a few years ago. Carol told me that when she'd get the information on Fridays about the next week's show and see that my mom was scheduled, she was always happy because she knew my mom could act and sing and that they were going to have a great time together.

My mom would appear on *The Carol Burnett Show* six times between 1970 and 1972. Some of the skits are hilarious even today. Others are a little painful to watch. Fat jokes were permissible if not encouraged in that era of television, even if the jabs were only insinuated. In one skit, Carol and my mom are sitting in a movie theater at a foreign film festival. As the films shift from one nationality to another, so do the snacks being devoured by the two women. As the skit progresses, the films shift quicker and quicker, as do the snacks being devoured. On other appearances, my mom sang with other guests such as Bernadette Peters. She even portrayed Mae West in one of the skits.

It was all seemingly good fun for the early 1970s, but I imagine playing the part of the Fat Girl had long ago become less funny to my mom. Still, she persevered and grinned through it all just as she always had.

As an only child growing up in a house that was constantly filled with my mother's friends, I spent most of my early years around adults. By the time I turned three in April 1970, I was lonely for other children to play with, so my mother decided to start me in preschool. Despite her rock and roll lifestyle, she enrolled me in a Jewish preschool at one of the local synagogues, Temple Isaiah in West Los Angeles. Between television tapings and recording sessions, my mom was often tied up in the afternoons, so my nanny, Virginia, was the one who typically picked me up from preschool and brought me home.

Right around this time, Leah became pregnant with my cousin Nathaniel. Finding an apartment to rent that allowed children had proven to be a challenge difficult to overcome, so Leah fixed up a bedroom area above my mom's garage. She and Russ moved in and stayed with us for a while. On one hot afternoon, Leah was upstairs in her room lying down with the window open. She could hear Virginia's car pull into the driveway, and as we exited, she could tell that Virginia was upset with me. I'd gotten my dress dirty at school that day, and Virginia was yelling at me, telling me I was a bad little girl for doing so. The tone and volume of Virginia's voice concerned Leah, who came downstairs to have a talk with her.

When my mother traveled for work, Leah took care of me on the weekends. Now she told the nanny to feel free to take that following Monday off, just for good measure.

That night as she was giving me my bath, Leah noticed a series of long, thin marks on my lower back and the backs of my legs.

"Owen, you have bruises on your back. How did they get there?" she asked.

"I fell," I quickly told her. Virginia must have told me to say this if anyone questioned the bruises.

Not believing me, Leah pressed further. "Are you sure? They look pretty bad."

Eventually, I disclosed that Virginia had been spanking me with a wooden spoon. At three years old, I was in the midst of being potty trained, and would wet my bed at night on occasion. Those were the days before disposable diapers, back in the era of cloth diapers and rubber pants. When a child was in the training stages, rubber sheets were used to protect the bed. When I had accidents during the night, Virginia would get angry and make me change my own sheets. I'm sure the beatings happened then. I also was still taking a bottle at night, which Virginia was determined to omit. I resorted to my thumb, becoming a chronic thumb sucker, which she also attempted to stop by coating my thumb in Tabasco hot sauce. But I would just go and wash off the spicy sauce in the nearby bathroom. I was no dummy.

Leah told my mother about the bruises when she got back, but by then all evidence of them was gone. I don't think my mom believed that I was in danger, although I was. Virginia stayed with us for a while longer. Eventually she left, but the damage had been done.

My mom continued to appear on various television, variety, and game shows of the era. She made her film debut in the children's fantasy movie *Pufnstuf* in June 1970. The film was produced by our neighbor Sid Krofft and his brother, Marty. She played the sister of Witchiepoo, the film's antagonist. Reclining in a white clawfoot bathtub filled with fruit, she sang the film's theme song, "Different," about recognizing and accepting one's differences as wonderful. Just as in "Make Your Own Kind of Music," the theme of acceptance was forefronted in her music again.

She was also immortalized in animation on an episode of the Saturday morning children's show *Scooby-Doo, Where Are You!* for which she even voiced her own character. Of all her many television appearances, this was the one that excited me most. I loved Scooby-Doo. But even in animated form, she couldn't escape being associated with food. Her character—aptly named "Cass Elliot"—owned a haunted candy factory that had been overrun by monsters, and she enlisted the help of Scooby-Doo and his gang to drive them out.

In 1970, my mother was approached about making a record with Dave Mason, formerly of Traffic. Mickey Shapiro, one of her attorneys, remembers that the idea to pair my mom with the English-born Mason was born out of a discussion he'd had with my mother's management team. Mason was a big star overseas, and his label, Blue Thumb, was looking for him to perform similarly in America. The opportunity to pair him with my mother seemed promising, since she had a proven track record with singing alongside other voices. It only took one conversation to convince her.

And that was it, Shapiro recalls. "Cass bought it in about five seconds," he said.

My mom co-wrote one of the songs—"Here We Go Again"—with her friend Bryan Garofalo. The soft rock style of the record suited her voice beautifully. She used a vocal recording technique known as "doubling." Doubling a vocal is achieved by layering the recorded tracks on top of one another to create the sound of two or more voices. It makes a voice sound fuller. The eponymous album *Dave Mason & Cass Elliot* was recorded in 1970 and released in March of 1971. Unfortunately, being poorly marketed, the album was not a success despite critical acclaim. This album is one that only the truly devoted of my mother's fans even know exists, making it a veritable cult classic.

In May of 1971, realizing that my mother's contracts with Dunhill/ABC were on the brink of expiration, one of my mother's managers, Hal Landers, consulted Mickey Shapiro to ask about securing a new recording contract for her. Mickey felt confident he would be able to make a deal for her, since he was well connected in the record business and had recently done a major deal with RCA Records for Wilson Pickett. RCA was looking for major stars to sign, and Mickey knew it. My mother was now an established, successful musical artist, and she wanted a deal that reflected this. To this end, they decided to ask for an exorbitant amount of money.

Mickey called Bob Summers, who was one of the heads of RCA at the time. The deal might just be "too rich" for them, Mickey said, but he nonetheless shared the terms they were looking for: six albums with a $900,000 per album fee, plus a $750,000 non-recoupable signing bonus. And a 20 percent royalty rate.

Bob paused, then replied, "We can't do a 20 percent royalty rate."

Holy shit, Mickey said to himself, when he realized this meant the rest of the deal could go through. His 5 percent commission would come to . . . well, a shitload of money for a newly divorced thirty-one-year-old attorney who was practically broke. Child support and alimony weren't cheap.

He reported back to Hal Landers and Bobby Roberts, who was also on my mother's management team.

"Are you kidding, Mickey? Let's get on a plane and *go!*" was their response.

So, the foursome flew to New York, where they checked into the Sherry-Netherland Hotel. Mickey says they all expected the deal to blow up in the office before it was inked, and Hal and Bobby didn't want to be there for that part. So only he and my mom rode down to the RCA offices on Forty-Fourth Street the following day.

"Your mom, your *mom* . . . is . . . you know . . . your *mother.*" Mickey laughs. "She's wearing a *schmatta*. Very unkempt. She didn't give a shit. We walk into the reception area of the RCA offices, and people start applauding. They'd never seen a real star before. We go into this room, and the guy there is SO nervous with the deal memo. He was literally shaking signing the contract and all of a sudden, the phone rings. I figure, *We're fucked. They've figured it out. They're gonna get slaughtered over this deal. It's over.*"

The guy answered his phone, and upon hanging up, asked Mickey and my mom if they wouldn't mind going upstairs to meet David Sarnoff, the chairman of RCA, who was known as "the General" because he had served as a brigadier general during World War II.

"I figured, we are *so* fucked," Mickey recalls. But of course, they said they'd meet him. "So we go upstairs to his giant office," he continues. "His desk was elevated, a United States flag, a big RCA logo behind him."

Sarnoff started the conversation, addressing my mother first, saying "Well, you know, ma'am, it's really a great honor to invite you to be a part of the RCA family."

Mickey must have released a huge exhale of relief.

Between the office's seating area and Sarnoff's desk, in a spot that was impossible to miss, was a platform that held a small statue of the mascot and logo of RCA Records, a dog named Nipper, who sat with his head tilted to the side, as if listening. The actual name of the statue was *His Master's Voice*, depicting the dog atop his owner's casket listening for the voice of his deceased master. The Nipper that resided in Sarnoff's office was *the* Nipper, the original that was used as one of the prototypes for all the other Nippers in existence.

My mother, for reasons never quite clear to anyone but her, decided this little dog statue was coming home with her. Always the prankster. When Sarnoff was briefly called out of the office, and Mickey was not paying attention, she sneakily slid Nipper under her dress.

Nobody was the wiser until they were in the limo on the way back to the Sherry-Netherland. Mickey was exalting in the afterglow of having just made a major deal that looked like it was actually going to go through when my mother chimed in.

"Look what I did," she said. She lifted her dress to reveal the statue of Nipper.

"Jesus, Cass!" Mickey shouted. *"What the fuck were you thinking?"*

She replied, "Well, it's kind of a joke . . ."

Except it also kind of wasn't. Mickey was now faced with a dilemma. His major new RCA star had just stolen RCA property. Not exactly the best way to start a new relationship.

Back at the hotel, Mickey consulted with Landers and Roberts who told him that of course he had to take Nipper back. *What am I going to say?* Mickey wondered. He directed the limo back to Forty-Fourth Street, where the theft had already been discovered. The building was on total lockdown. Armed guards, the whole thing. Mickey got out of the car, Nipper in hand. The guards escorted him back upstairs where Sarnoff was waiting.

"Sir. Sir," Mickey sputtered. "Cass was so excited about being a part of the RCA family, she wanted me to take it across the street to Tiffany's and have it dipped in platinum."

"That is the worst story I've ever heard," Sarnoff replied.

Nonetheless, the deal went through. And as Mickey recalls, "When I went back, I told your mother, and she was laughing her head off."

"That must have been fun for you," she said.

"It wasn't," he remembers. "But she thought it was hilarious."

Coincidentally, 1971 also found the Mamas and the Papas reunited, though not necessarily by choice. Each member had received an individual letter from Dunhill/ABC Records stating that unless the group provided the company with another album of new material, they would be in breach of contract and in debt to Dunhill/ABC for a cool $1 million. This meant that they needed to get back to work together, which they did. Begrudgingly.

John, Michelle, Denny, and my mom headed back into the studio in June of 1971 to record the album that would be called *People Like Us*. As John later wrote in his 1986 autobiography, *Papa John*, "The *People Like Us* sessions were efficient but perfunctory. It was rare we were all together [in the studio]. Most tracks were dubbed, one vocal at a time. The material was too laid-back and failed to make maximum use of Cass's voice. I spent hundreds of hours splicing tape together and creating an illusion of "live" harmony. We had been apart now for as long as we had been together. The elegance, the fire, the graceful union of our voices were long gone."

In his one-man musical, Denny looked back on those weeks with a melancholy twist:

After one of the sessions—Michelle has left with Jack Nicholson and John's in the booth wired and mixing up a storm, and I'm just holding up the wall when Cass comes over and says:

"What's the matter, Dennis?"

"Aw, Cass, it all just floated away."

"Floated away? Dennis, they hauled it away in trucks and nobody is ever going to tell us where they put it."

That night I drove her home and we cracked a bottle of Jack Daniel's Green Label and lay on the bed talking and watching the tube and . . . what happened that night is nobody's business. In the morning she made a marvelous breakfast of croissants and blueberries and after that she headed out, back on the road.

He left it at that, a gentleman to his core.

CHAPTER 8

THE ONE SINGLE RELEASED FROM *PEOPLE LIKE US*, "Step Out," only reached number eighty-one on the *Billboard* Hot 100, and the album stiffed. The Mamas and the Papas were, in effect, done with one another.

Almost immediately upon finishing *People Like Us*, my mom headed into RCA's studios on Sunset Boulevard in Los Angeles with producer Lew Merenstein. Merenstein had recently been involved in the Van Morrison record *Moondance*, and now he was working with my mom on her first solo effort for RCA, titled simply *Cass Elliot*.

Her new contract with RCA gave her much more artistic freedom than she'd been able to enjoy as part of the Mamas and the Papas, or with Dunhill for that matter, and she relished this opportunity. Under the new agreement, my mom would finally be able to unilaterally choose and record songs that moved her and spoke to her. She must have been over the moon. Once again, she included a song penned by her sister,

Leah, "When It Doesn't Work Out." She also recorded a song by Judee Sill, "Jesus Was a Cross Maker," and a song by her friend Bruce Johnston. Bruce's song "Disney Girls" had originally been performed by the Beach Boys, whom Bruce had begun touring with.

When the time came to record the album, Bruce came to the studio to add vocals and brought along Carl Wilson of the Beach Boys. They both sang on the background parts with my mom and were credited on the album as the Hi Beach Mamas. The end results were beautiful, haunting vocals, with my mother's lead sounding almost as if she's nearly in tears.

The RCA recording sessions were completed by mid-November of 1971. For the album cover, renowned Hollywood photographer George Hurrell captured my mother in black and white. Hurrell had been a preeminent glamour studio photographer, shooting everyone from Clark Gable to Jean Harlow as the head of portrait photography at MGM before going out on his own. His picture of my mom, with her hand resting on the side of her face and her heavy gold bracelets on her arm, is one of the most stunning pictures ever taken of her. Dressed to the nines, with a feather boa around her neck and her head tilted slightly, she was in her element. He made her look beautiful. She must have felt beautiful, too, and it shows.

Advertisements in the music business trade magazines like *Billboard* and *Cashbox* were purchased and circulated in advance of the release to create a buzz. Ads for the album used

My grandparents, Philip and Bessie Cohen, with my mom at age five. (Courtesy of the estate of Cass Elliot)

Mom, with a different look, her little hands thrust into her pants pockets. (Courtesy of the estate of Cass Elliot)

My grandmother and mom on the beach. I think my mom is around seven here. My grandma in a bikini? (Courtesy of the estate of Cass Elliot)

My mom holding her baby sister, Leah, in 1942.
(Courtesy of the estate of Cass Elliot)

Leah, 13, and baby brother Joey, 9. (Courtesy of th
estate of Cass Elliot)

My mother, with the spotlight shining on her, with The Mugwumps. From left, my mom,
Jim Hendricks, Tim Rose, and Denny Doherty. (Courtesy of the estate of Cass Elliot)

The Mamas and the Papas, photoshoot for *Rolling Stone*, in my playhouse. (© Henry Diltz)

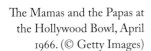

The Mamas and the Papas at the Hollywood Bowl, April 1966. (© Getty Images)

Unaware of the musical magic occurring behind me, I am engrossed in playing with a metal film canister. From left, Joni Mitchell with her guitar, David Crosby with his joint, and Eric Clapton, watching Joni play intently. (© Henry Diltz)

Mom and me at the Renaissance Pleasure Faire in 1968. I love the way she's looking at me; she looks so proud. I was blissful in her arms (© Henry Diltz)

My mom and Leah at my second birthday party at our home in Laurel Canyon. Sisters. The family resemblance is uncanny. (© Henry Diltz)

After I'd had my way with the cake and ice cream, I needed a wipe down from Mom, who obviously loved it, by the look on her face! (© Henry Diltz)

After my post-cake makeover, with my aunt Leah. (© Henry Diltz)

Truly one of my favorite shots of my mom, cracking up. (© Henry Diltz)

My great grandmother, Chaya, my grandma Bess, and me at home in Los Angeles. (Courtesy of Leah Kunkel)

Naked in the daisies for the short-lived *Cheetah* magazine, this is another one of my favorite pictures. Absolutely beautiful. (© by Jerry Schatzberg)

Guest-hosting for Johnny Carson on the *Tonight Show*, January 1973. She's deep in conversation here with the guest. I bet she was a fantastic interviewer and host. (© Getty Images)

Graham Nash snapped this photo of my mom on the phone at our house in Laurel Canyon. He really captured her in her element. (© Graham Nash)

Before Nathaniel and I moved to Massachusetts in 1981, we had pictures taken with Russ in Los Angeles. I'd just had a perm. (© Randee St Nicholas)

Nathaniel, Leah, and me in Los Angeles, 1996. (© Henry Diltz)

The Mamas and the Papas kids, for *People* magazine in 1997. Top row from left, Mackenzie Phillips, John Doherty, Aron Wilson, Bijou Phillips, Jeffrey Phillips, Jessica Doherty. Middle row from left, Emberly Doherty, Chynna Phillips, yours truly. Reclining on floor, Austin Hines. (© Neal Preston)

Backstage at the Rock and Roll Hall of Fame induction ceremony, Waldorf Astoria Hotel in New York, 1998. The look on my face isn't fear; it's pain. Those. Boots. Were. Horrible. (© Getty Images)

On October 3, 2022, celebrating the star installation on the Hollywood Walk of Fame. From left, John Sebastian, me, Leah, Michelle Phillips, and Stephen Stills. What an amazing day. (© Getty Images)

Deliriously happy, sitting next to my mom's star. It felt like a dream come true, and I knew my mom would've been over the moon. (© Getty Images)

Leah and me, on the day of the star installation. (© Getty Images)

the Hurrell portrait with the copy "Mama is home. Free." It was followed by text in a smaller font: "Here's Cass. Out front where she belongs. A new career, a new album, and a new single, 'Baby I'm Yours.' And a new label."

"Baby I'm Yours" was released on February 25, 1972, with "Cherries Jubilee" on the B side. A second single, "That Song," was released in April of 1972. On the B side of this single was Leah's song "When It Doesn't Work Out."

Leah and Russ had by this time welcomed their son, Nathaniel, who was now a toddler. They had moved out of our house in the Hollywood Hills and into an apartment by the beach in Malibu. I'd visit them at their new place and play in the concrete area that was out in the back of their apartment, while the clean smell of ocean air surrounded me. Malibu seemed exotic and distant to a five-year-old. I hadn't seen much of the world beyond Los Angeles, but that was about to change.

After "That Song" failed to register on any charts, just like the previous two singles, it was decided that perhaps a change of scenery was in order for the next album. My mother loved to travel, and this was a perfect opportunity for her to do that and make a record at the same time. London was chosen as the destination, with the recording to take place at the legendary Trident Studios in Soho. Trident was where the Beatles had recorded "Hey Jude" and where, in later years, David Bowie would record *The Rise and Fall of Ziggy Stardust and the Spiders from Mars.*

My mom had always loved London and had felt a special connection to the place. In a 1968 *Rolling Stone* interview she said she believed she'd been British in a past life. She even said that at one point she'd visited Stonehenge and had the strong sensation that she'd been there before. The same thing had happened when she visited the Tower of London.

Now she was headed back to England in the summer of 1972, with me and a nanny in tow. A townhouse was rented for us to stay in for the duration of our trip. I was five years old, learning to count, and I remember being in awe of how *many* stairs were in this house, which had only two or three rooms per floor. The kitchen was all the way downstairs, even below the floor where the front door was. The ten different sets of stairs in the townhouse seemed like a whole lot to me, and it took around eight sets of those steps for me to get from the kitchen all the way to the floor where my mom's room was. All ten sets of stairs took me to the very top of the house. My room and my nanny's room were on the top floor and my mom was right below us.

When my mom was at work, the nanny and I explored London. We went to see the changing of the guard at Buckingham Palace, where I became impatient waiting for the event to begin. I'm not sure if we stayed, because I'm pretty sure that I threw a fit. I remember thinking to myself, "This is silly. What are we waiting around this long for?"

About a mile from Buckingham Palace, over at Trident Studios, my mom was recording the album *The Road Is No*

Place for a Lady. The album's title track was another song written by Leah, and the rest were handpicked by my mom. Other songs on the album included one by her new friend, singer, songwriter, and actor Paul Williams, titled simply "Say Hello." As with so many of the songs that she picked to record, the lyrics to "Say Hello" spoke of unity and understanding.

> *Let's take some time and get to know one another*
> *We'll solve our problems if we do*
> *We may be different, but we won't know till we try*
> *You learn from me, and I'll learn from you*

Before we left London, the songs were mixed and their final versions decided upon. The process of mixing a song involves taking all of the recorded instruments and vocals and balancing out the levels. It was a complicated, drawn-out process done on a mixing console at a professional recording studio.

The best analogy I can offer to convey the importance of a proper mix is one of a car with four tires. If any of the tires loses pressure, the car will not drive smoothly. They all need to be inflated and balanced correctly. The same is true for mixing a song. The instruments and the vocals must be in perfect balance to be pleasing to the ear.

When a song was recorded in those days, it was recorded on an analog tape recorder. The tape itself was physically wound into and around the tape machine's heads, and each track was individually adjusted one by one, using a tiny screwdriver.

Usually this was the job of the lowly second engineer, and it was a long, arduous process, but one that was imperative every time a new tape was put up onto the machine for recording or for playback.

Unbeknownst to my mom's producer, Lew Merenstein, in the days that followed the completion of the album's recording, another client had used the studio and the equipment. So, when the time came to do the mixes, nobody on my mother's team checked to make sure the tape was still aligned properly for their project.

The result was an album that sounded awful. When Merenstein played the final versions to the executives back in New York at RCA, he was horrified by what emanated from the speakers in the offices.

The first single designated for release was "(If You're Gonna) Break Another Heart." The vocals were set far too low and muffled, and the bass was so prevalent that it sounded as if the bass player had mixed the record to spotlight his performance only.

Merenstein told the executives that he would go back to London, since the primary tapes of the record were still overseas, to remix the single immediately. He asked them to be patient and not to release the single in its current form.

When my mom and I returned to Los Angeles in midsummer of 1972, preparations were already being made for the album's release. The cover photo was taken on the railroad tracks next to a parked dining car at Griffith Park's Travel

Town Museum in Burbank. My mother reclined on a yellow velvet Victorian-era sofa in a mock living room set up on the tracks. She looked relaxed and glamorous on the comfortable furniture, like she hadn't a care in the world. On the outside, anyway. In truth, she was always on the go, always working. As a single mom, she had little choice.

Later that year, on September 25, my mom and I did a guest slot on Dinah Shore's daytime variety talk show *Dinah's Place*. Wearing a navy-blue dress adorned with a sailor's collar with a multicolored rhinestone USA brooch pinned to her shoulder, my mom chatted with Dinah in the first segment, mostly about her recent forty-pound weight loss and her latest diet tips. She quipped that she'd been dieting for so long in her life that all she needed to do was to *look* at something and know how many calories were in it. I'm sure that publicly discussing her weight was never something that she felt good about, but Dinah Shore was a sweet Southern woman at her core, and my mother seemed to be comfortable discussing it on her show. Woman to woman.

Dinah asked my mom what she liked to do when she wasn't traveling for work. Play with me, she said. As a working mother, she explained, she relished her time at home. "I read a little bit, I crochet a little bit, and I watch television. Then, I go out and carouse and burn down buildings," she said, laughing along with Dinah. I find her comment hysterically funny. My mom sure had a sarcastic, dry humor. My favorite kind.

They also discussed the origin of my name. My mother explained that she'd been reading a Welsh book when she was pregnant with me and had seen a name—Branwyn—that she'd liked but rejected as a bit "unwieldy." She didn't have a name picked out for me when I was born, but upon being told she had to name me before leaving the hospital, she'd hastily picked "Owen."

"Then I really liked it," she admitted.

It had sort of a peaceful sound, she said, and Dinah agreed, saying I was that kind of person. Peaceful. (Why does that strike me as so funny now? Like, have we met?)

"I must tell you this," Dinah said, addressing the in-studio audience. "When I asked Cass to do the show, I said, 'Do you suppose Owen would come on?' and you said, 'I'll ask her.' So, you did ask her, and thank heavens she said okay. And I was delighted, but so you consult her on many things, don't you?"

My mother replied, "Well, anything that I feel involves our family. For instance, she said to me . . . a couple of weeks ago, 'You know, Mom, all I need is a couple of brothers and three sisters.'"

Dinah chuckled, and my mother continued, "I said, 'Wow that's a lot,' and explained to her that in order for us to have any more children, I would have to be married, and she said, 'Well, can't we find a man?' and I said, 'Well, I don't know if I want to get married again,' and we talked about that for a while." At her core, my mom apparently still had the picket fence fantasy in her head, just as society had taught her. "Then

I tried to explain it to her," she went on. "I asked her why it was important to her. She told me that then the other child would have someone to play with."

I have a faint memory of that conversation, just my mom and me. I remember wandering into her room one afternoon, bored. She was sitting on her bed, watching television. I did what I usually would do and flopped down on her bed next to her. I figured I'd ask her about my idea about acquiring some brothers and sisters. If I had someone to play with on a day like this one, I wouldn't be bored, was my thought.

My mom continued, "I thought that was a valid point and I told her that, and then we started discussing the fact that there are a lot of children that don't have homes or mommies or daddies and that maybe we could invite one of them to come and live with us. Now she's deciding about that, and if that would be agreeable to her, I would love to adopt a child. But I think she should be consulted; it's her home too."

Many years later, when I was sent a VHS tape of the show and saw it for the first time, I was pleasantly surprised and at the same time sad to discover that had she lived a longer life, she might have adopted one or more children and maybe I'd have had siblings to grow up with. It was just one more example of how different life might have been for her, and for me.

Dinah had arranged for a gardening segment, complete with a project for me to do while she and my mom talked more. But first, Dinah had a few questions for five-year-old me. "You went to Europe with Mommy not too long ago?" Dinah asked me.

I was standing by my mother's side dressed in a dark dress with a Peter Pan collar, with matching white barrettes holding back my honey-colored shoulder-length hair.

"Right," I said. I twisted my tongue around in my mouth, experimenting with how it felt. I didn't realize that thousands, maybe millions, of people were watching me do it.

"Did you enjoy it?"

"Yeah."

"You're glad to be home now, huh?"

"Yeah."

"You're going to be a great interview, Owen," Dinah laughed.

My mom put her arm around me and held me close as Dinah explained my gardening project. I was to take potting soil from one container and transfer it into a larger container. Simple enough, right? The only problem was that I worked faster than they talked and was done before they were finished talking. Noticing this, I began to reverse what I had already done, putting the soil *back* into its original container.

My green thumb began and ended right there, on that soundstage somewhere in Los Angeles. Even today, fifty years later, I kill every houseplant, without fail.

Even though RCA had assured Merenstein they would wait for a remix, the label chose to release *The Road Is No Place for a Lady* in its initial form in August of 1972. The flawed cut of

"(If You're) Gonna Break Another Heart" with "Disney Girls," a song from my mom's previous album, on the B side, failed to chart with any success. While this wasn't great news, there was always the next album to look forward to.

That summer of 1972 was a crucible for my mother, artistically, professionally, and politically all at once. It was a presidential election year, and the Democratic convention took place in Miami that July. She was backing the Democratic Party's candidate, Senator George McGovern of South Dakota. The country was at a crossroads. On June 17, five men had been arrested in the offices of the Democratic Committee Headquarters at the Watergate Hotel. Two days later, it was revealed that one of the individuals arrested was the Republican Party security chief for the Committee to Re-Elect the President, though it would take two more years for evidence of President Nixon's participation to be revealed.

My mother had always been interested in politics and current events. She'd become even more passionate about the state of our nation's affairs after I was born. She told Mike Douglas on a visit to his show in 1972,

> My child is going to be living, with G-d's help, long after I'm gone, and I would like to know that it's going to be a nice place for her to live in. And it's my job and the job of all of us to make it happen now, so we don't dump the mess into our kids' laps that we are fighting with now. I don't want to turn around when she's twenty and say, "I'm sorry about the way

things are in the world." That's essentially what our parents sent us. But we can only give our children the benefit of what we know. My daughter may find things I believe in myself untrue for her, but I still must provide her with a frame of reference until she's ready to go out and find a frame of reference for herself. She is going to be around for a long while, and so am I. When she's ready I'll know.

Publicly, she was characteristically vocal about issues she thought needed to be addressed in the country. In 1972, the state of the government was deplorable, and she was eager to use her platform to get the word out to the masses to vote for the things that they felt were important. She knew that using her position as a celebrity brought with it great responsibility, and she wasn't shy about using it. That's a part of her history and her personality I've always been proud of. She was a Levine woman, through and through.

In August, she co-hosted the pilot episode of a new show called *The Midnight Special* along with John Denver. The voting age had been lowered from twenty-one to eighteen the previous year, and this election cycle was the first time this new right would be exercised. The show was geared toward younger viewers and intended to get them out to vote. It was an exciting time, and the young people of the country were fired up.

Before beginning the song together, my mom and Denver chatted for a few minutes about the importance of voting. My mom said that she'd been traveling around the country for the past few months talking to the kids on college campuses and learning about the things that they felt were important. She'd discovered that many Americans were apathetic in regard to the state of the country, and she'd told people that in order to effect any sort of change, that the answer was getting out and voting. It was the American way, and the only way.

In September of 1972, my mom went on a three-day campaign tour for George McGovern. As part of the learning materials, the campaign sent out three-ring notebooks to volunteers that included all the information needed to get up to date on current issues and understand where the candidates stood on those issues. Of all the somewhat bizarre possessions of my mother's that were saved, this notebook was one of them, with its various notes and travel itineraries intact. One of the items tucked inside was a small index card, with thoughts and ideas for a speech written in my mother's hand.

"By inauguration day, 1973, it will have been nearly a decade since the country was accustomed to believing its President," she had written.

"Wouldn't it be nice to wake up in the morning and like the President?"

"The Republican Party is running the "office" (the President) rather than Nixon."

I'm struck by how honest and true these three statements were. I also believe each of these statements. My mom was passionate about how the country was being run. I think of her sobbing alone in the back of the Hootenanny bus when she learned of JFK's assassination, so overcome by loss and despair. JFK's assassination had been a rude awakening for most Americans, and my mom believed the involvement of younger voters was certain to make a difference in how future elections would shape the country in the years ahead. She wasn't wrong about that.

I've wondered how she'd feel about the current state of politics. I haven't had to wonder for long.

"She'd be appalled," Stephen Stills said, very simply, when I asked him. I'd have to agree with that sentiment totally.

CHAPTER 9

MY MOM'S ROOM WAS DOWN THE HALL FROM MINE, just past the upstairs bathroom at the top of the stairs. When she was at home, which wasn't a whole lot, I'd wander in and flop down on her bed with her to talk. One afternoon, I came in after school, frustrated. I told her that I wanted to change my first name to Ellen. After all, I carefully explained to her, most people thought I was *saying* "Ellen" when I said "Owen," and I was really tired of having to repeat my name over and over again. I had *no* idea then that my mom's given name was Ellen. I'm sure that must have been an interesting moment for her, hearing me say I wanted my name to be Ellen. She patiently explained to me that she thought that when I was older, I'd appreciate the uniqueness of my name.

On another afternoon, my mom was in her room watching the TV set at the foot of her gigantic bed. My mother was a sports fan and loved to watch football. Sitting with her one day, I tried to figure out what was so interesting about watching these guys running after a ball on a big field. I asked her what she liked so much about watching football. She replied that the players' "tushies looked so cute in the tight white pants." I nodded in agreement as if I understood, but I had zero idea what she truly meant.

The flawed release of *The Road Is No Place for a Lady* failed to bring much commercial success, if any. The tides of music were changing again. The distinctive folk rock of the sixties and early seventies had begun morphing into the midseventies style of soft rock. Groups like Crosby, Stills & Nash and the Eagles were riding the radio airwaves. My mom no doubt observed these winds of change and decided it was time to make some of her own.

First, she cut ties with Bobby Roberts, who had been managing her since he'd managed the Mamas and the Papas. Allan Carr was the right person to guide her new direction and career, she believed. He'd managed the careers of Hollywood luminaries like Tony Curtis and Peter Sellers and was currently managing Ann-Margret as well.

Allan was a flamboyant gay man of diminutive stature and was known about town for his flashy Hollywood parties and his many connections in show business. He knew *everyone*. My mother hired him in the winter of 1972, and he promptly got to work figuring out her new direction. She wasn't a rock and roll singer at her core, though she'd successfully become one to be part of the Mamas and the Papas. What really made her tick, though, were large productions featuring string sections and orchestrations. With my mother's love for cabaret-style performances, another stab at a successful nightclub act was determined to be the next logical step.

Meanwhile, my mom continued to work in television, appearing as guest host for Johnny Carson on January 29, 1973. The first segment of that show featured actor Tony Curtis, who spoke with her about his family and his art. She knew some things about the latter, she confessed. She'd recently visited his home with Allan Carr, on a day when Tony and Janet Leigh, his wife, were both sick in bed. So, she'd freely wandered around their house, admiring the decor and all of the art on her own. That was certainly a gutsy thing to have done.

But then in mid-March of that year, my mom slipped on some water on the kitchen floor of our house. The fall resulted in a fairly serious injury to her knee, requiring surgery to repair it. She would need to spend some time in bed afterward to recuperate. Initially placed into a cast following the operation, she wouldn't be able to use the stairs for a while. A hospital bed was rented for her and placed in the den, where a television had also been set up. Coming home one day after school, I went into the den to see her. "Come here," she said, patting the bed next to her. "Come watch this movie with me." It was *The Wizard of Oz*, which I had never seen before. We watched it together, me for the first time, and her for G-d only knows how many times. Every time I see the movie now, even today, I hold in my heart that the first time I saw the movie, it was with my mom. She missed so many of my "firsts," and knowing that we at least had that one makes me feel good.

For her new nightclub act, arranger Marvin Laird was hired along with choreographer Walter Painter. Both men were involved in choosing the songs to be performed. They sent their choices to Allan Carr for approval, and then to my mom. In addition to the new material, they wanted her to include some of the Mamas and the Papas songs that people knew her for, like "Dream a Little Dream of Me." They weren't wrong about that, but to devote a big chunk of her solo cabaret act to songs she'd done with a prior rock band didn't seem like the right choice to her, either. She needed to be convinced.

A compromise was struck. The final version of the cabaret show had her doing a medley of the Mamas and the Papas songs, using only a few verses and choruses from each. She would also do a few cover songs, like "My Love," written by her friend Paul McCartney about his wife, Linda. And of course, she would include some of her solo material, like "Make Your Own Kind of Music."

She also included the song that had been written exclusively for and about her, "Don't Call Me Mama Anymore," which addressed the frustration that my mother felt at being continually referred to as "Mama" Cass. She very much wanted to shed the moniker and expand her career as an artist in her own right, using the name she'd chosen for herself rather than one she had adopted for commercial purposes when she was only twenty-two years old.

"Don't Call Me Mama Anymore" was penned by her friend Earl Brown, and the lyrics sounded just like words my mom herself would have spoken.

You can call me honey, you can call me pal
I'll be your buddy buddy, maybe even be your gal
But don't call me mama anymore
Oh, you can call me fancy, you can call me plain
If I should call ya Tarzan, then you can call me Jane
But don't, don't call me mama anymore

Lord knows I know some folks refer to me
As good old Mama Cass
Ah, but that was then, and now is now
And I'd like to give that handle a Pasadena

Call me Julie Andrews, Peggy Lee, or Lucy Ball
Baby darlings, you can call me anything at all
But don't, don't call me mama anymore

You can call me partner, you can call me Ma'am
If your wife don't understand you, and you're smashed—
*   my name is Sam*
But don't, don't call me mama anymore

Call me Miss or Mrs., Betty Boop or Minnie Mouse
And you can call me Madam even though this ain't the house
But don't, don't call me mama anymore

Oh-oh-oh-oh-oh, if you come down with a fever
I'll be glad to hold ya hand
I make chicken soup that's really like no other
Well, I'm phoning you in hope that we'll be lifelong friends
But precious I don't wanna be your mother

'Cause I've done that before and was really rather good at it

You can call me swinger—it ain't true but what the hell
Call me fancy singer and you'll really ring my bell
But don't, don't call me mama anymore

I'll be your pet, your poopsie, your poochie, your peach
Your partner in crime
But in case you just forgot let me tell you one more time
Don't, don't you dare call me mama anymore

You can call me Cass

When it was determined the show was ready, she took me with her to Chicago for two days in July of 1973 so she could record the live album at Mister Kelly's. I was accustomed to being backstage and to being surrounded by adults, but I was also a typical six-year-old. Before the show began, I wandered over to the craft services buffet tables where I found a cup of cherry-flavored Jell-O. Just before the show began, I was informed that I was not allowed to bring the Jell-O into the audience. I became incredibly upset at the thought of leaving my sweet treat behind. Although I secretly wanted nothing more than that Jell-O, I resolved myself to sitting in my seat like I was supposed to. I knew the routine by then. I'd sit and watch the show with whoever was watching me that night. Me and Jell-O would meet up again later, of that I was certain.

When we returned to LA, my mother got a call from her friend Chuck Barris. Barris, by now a prominent TV producer, had a current hit with *The Dating Game*. He had produced my mother's first television special for ABC back in 1969, and they had remained friends ever since. They had even dated a couple of times, with Barris standing her up on at least one occasion.

His shitty behavior had prompted my mother to take a pen to our newly plastered living room wall and scrawl the following words in huge letters: "*Who does Chuck Barris think he is anyway?*" What began as my mother expressing her frustration at the lowly Barris started a tradition at 7708 Woodrow Wilson that lasted for the rest of our tenure at the house. Friends were encouraged to add their names, opinions, and thoughts to the wall over the years. The signatures and quotes added to the wall were reportedly legendary, but there were no pictures taken at the time to capture it in all its glory.

Now Barris wanted her to come on *The Dating Game*, and to bring my grandmother along as well. Grandma Bess was excited by the invitation and my mom wanted to make her mother happy, so she begrudgingly agreed to do it. As she would later tell Johnny Carson during an interview segment on his show, "I know all these people at *The Dating Game*; I've been hanging around there for years, surely they'll pick out three hot dudes . . . [but] they were the *lamest* and I was so mad. I thought 'how can you do this to me? I'm your *friend*! I came on your show to do you a favor and you're giving me these losers!' I didn't even go on the date. They say, 'dates with celebrities are subject to their availability' and I don't know, I just haven't been available," she said in a voice dripping with sarcasm.

Around the same time, my mom teamed up with Allan Carr to form a production company they cleverly named "Caloric Productions," and they fashioned an idea for a variety-style television special. The script for this special, which they called "Don't Call Me Mama Anymore," reads almost like a day-in-the-life format, with candid scenes to be shot in my mother's "dressing room" backstage. It closely resembled what reality television looks like today. All of the hustle and bustle that happens behind the scenes were dramatized and satirized for the benefit of the viewer at home. Of course, like "reality" television, it would be shot on a set that was made to look like an actual backstage dressing room, if actual backstage dressing rooms were professionally lit.

In the rear section of this "dressing room" was a small kitchen set where my Grandma Bess pretended to cook chicken soup. Grandma, who'd launched a second, sideline career as an actress, had recently filmed her first commercial, cast as "Mama Cass's Mama" to hawk Chung King Chinese Food. She'd appeared alongside the spokesman for the brand, wearing one of her signature brightly colored muumuus and looking like she'd just stepped off a cruise ship in Miami Beach.

"Don't Call Me Mama Anymore" was shot at CBS Television Center in Hollywood from September 10 to 12, 1973. The guests included Broadway singer Joel Grey and television icon Dick Van Dyke. Also appearing on the show was my mom's old friend Michelle Phillips. Michelle and my mom did a funny skit as waitresses in a restaurant, singing a rendition of the Mamas and the Papas tune "Monday, Monday" as "Tuesday, Tuesday." Dick Van Dyke and my mom did a sort of mashup performance of *Romeo and Juliet* and *Laurel and Hardy* with a misunderstanding of who was going to play who. My mother comes out on Juliet's balcony, dressed as Stan Laurel, and Dick Van Dyke comes out as Romeo, standing below. Hilarious. Van Dyke did the lines from *Romeo and Juliet*, and my mom responded as if she were Stan Hardy, in full character.

The skit with Joel Grey, singer and dancer extraordinaire, had him and my mom walking around the CBS Television Center, seemingly after hours, on dark and silent sets. As they walked through one of the stages, they saw one area that was lit, illuminating an old upright piano. As they approached, they recognized it as the piano used in the hit CBS TV show *All in the Family*. Grey took a seat on the piano's bench. He patted the seat next to him and began to play the opening notes to the already iconic *All in the Family* theme song, "Those Were the Days," but at a much slower pace than usual. The two of them sang a beautiful version of the theme before breaking into a short, intimate, cheek-to-cheek dance.

The week before the special was to air, my mom made her eighth appearance on *The Tonight Show* to promote both her new album and the TV special, which were being released simultaneously. She'd been a frequent guest on the show for many years, dating back to her first appearance in 1963 as part of the Big 3, during the show's New York days. Over the past ten years she'd become friendly with Johnny Carson and had even stepped in as a guest host a few times when he was on vacation. In the process, she'd become one of the first women to host a late-night talk show, sitting behind Johnny's desk as if it were her own. She was *so good* at it. She was a natural at conducting an intelligent conversation.

In total, she appeared on the show nine times over an eleven-year period. On this particular visit in September of 1973, she and Johnny spent the first few minutes chatting about the fall in our kitchen that had injured her knee. She joked that she'd been such an avid football fan, she'd now joined the club with torn cartilage like football players so often endured. Now she was using a cane to help her walk steadily with her knee weak in its recovery.

Johnny then went on to ask about a recent event in Baltimore, my mother's hometown. My mother confirmed that yes, the city had proclaimed Cass Elliot Day on August 15, 1973. There had been a parade in her honor and the mayor of Baltimore had given her the key to the city. He also bestowed upon my mother her long-awaited high school diploma, replete with a cap-and-gown ceremony so she could "graduate" in public. Grandma Bess sat beside her in the convertible car during the parade and proudly adjusted my mother's cap and gown on stage as my mom received her diploma. Mom, in her trademark sailor dress, her hair in low pigtails, stood next to the mayor and grinned. As the mayor presented her with an official honorary diploma from Forest Park High School, he announced her name as Ellen Naomi Cohen to the crowd. When she watched the footage from that day on *The Tonight Show* with Johnny, when the mayor read "Ellen Naomi Cohen," my mother quipped, "Oops. That's the real name!" It wasn't a known fact that "Cass" wasn't her legal name. Perhaps it had even been her secret until then.

After the back and forth with Johnny Carson, she performed "I'm Coming to the Best Part of My Life" from the new album live in the television studio along with the music track of the song. As she sang, she swayed in time to the beat in her black chiffon dress with dramatic bell-shaped sleeves. As the title of the song suggests, the lyrics told the story of reaching the pinnacle of one's success and enjoying every moment of it. I heard this song for the first time when I was nineteen, and instantly became emotional hearing my mother sing the words, "I'm coming to the best part of my life," while simultaneously knowing how soon after recording that song her life would end. I'm not a cryer, really. I don't remember crying at her funeral, even, but the irony of those lyrics just slayed me.

The *Don't Call Me Mama Anymore* television special aired on September 28, 1973, to rave reviews. The executives at CBS were pleased, and there were mentions in the trade magazines about the possibility of my mom being brought onboard as a summer replacement for the Sonny and Cher timeslot. The vice president of CBS confirmed in one of the trade magazines that there were talks underway.

All of those rehearsals and subsequent taping of the *Don't Call Me Mama Anymore* special had been extensive. She'd had the knee operation only five months before undertaking the rehearsal process. After the two days of taping and a little dancing, she was back to using her cane full time. In an interview with Marilyn Beck of the *San Francisco Examiner*, she told Marilyn that healing had been a long process due to her weight, but that she'd lost forty-five pounds in the months of bedrest and rehabilitation that followed the surgery. She was exhausted, and now her knee hurt. She checked into the hospital to rest for a few days on the advice of her doctors at the beginning of October.

November found my mother booked into the Venetian Room at the Fairmont Hotel in San Francisco, with her cane in tow. She was obviously still healing, and did the three-day engagement mostly seated while she sang and chatted comfortably with the audience.

On December 7, 1973, she appeared on NBC's *Dean Martin Show* for a celebrity roast of actor Carroll O'Connor, television's faithful grouch Archie Bunker. She was one of the few women among a long cast list of men, including Don Rickles, Gene Kelly, Joey Bishop, Redd Foxx, and Nipsey Russell, and together they roasted O'Connor with pure hilarity. Introducing her, Martin said, "Cass Elliot is truly a great entertainer; I love that gal. I wouldn't say she's fat, but from the front she looks like Carroll O'Connor from the back. Only kidding. Ladies and gentlemen, the lovely Cass Elliot."

Stepping up to the microphone, my mom unleashed her dry wit. Commenting immediately that she was the *only* woman on the dais, she proceeded to chide O'Connor for his less-than-wonderful treatment of his television wife, the meek but extraordinarily loved Edith Bunker, never even opening a car door for her. Carroll got up to give her a hug and a kiss as she finished her speech. Announcing that he was the recipient of the First Annual Male Chauvinist Pig Award, she bent down and got his award for him, a Golden Pig statue mounted on a wooden base.

The crowd roared with laughter. They loved it. She really knocked it out of the park that night.

December wasn't over yet, and she was due to perform in Honolulu, Hawaii, at a club called C'est Si Bon. But when she arrived, she felt unwell with flu symptoms and was taken to the hospital there, missing part of her engagement as a result. Because she was hospitalized for six days, the original two-week booking ended up becoming only a three-night gig.

The *Honolulu Advertiser* sent a reporter to interview my mom after she'd been released from the hospital and was recuperating in the penthouse suite at the Pacific Beach Hotel. Among the things they talked about was my mother's love life. She spoke of a serious boyfriend that she said she'd been going with for the last five years, a man named Chris Conroy. Chris was an aviation executive, she told the *Advertiser* reporter. I've racked my memory to no avail. I don't remember him, although I think that if he'd truly been that important to her, I would have.

As she chatted with the reporter, they walked onto the balcony and my mom pointed to me, playing on the beach below with other children. Whenever she had to travel for work, she always made me part of the plan. Part of the deal, one could surmise, and almost written into the contract. She loved me *that* much.

CHAPTER 10

I N JANUARY OF 1974, I WENT BACK TO THE FIRST GRADE and my mom flew to Cincinnati for twelve nights at the Beverly Hills Supper Club. Even though I usually traveled with her, now that I was older, my mom—herself the studious type—must have not wanted me to miss school. When she came home from Cincinnati, she went right into rehearsals for a European tour Allan had booked for her that summer, beginning with a two-week engagement at London's Palladium Theater in July.

The plan was to spruce up the previous year's *Don't Call Me Mama Anymore* show by adding a song or two. A rehearsal space was rented in the San Fernando Valley section of Los Angeles. Choreographer Walter Painter and musical director Marvin Laird were brought back to work on the show. Two young male singer-dancers were hired.

When I interviewed Walter and Marvin recently, I asked them both the same question. "Do you think my mom was happy? Do you think she was excited?" I've been searching for this answer for decades.

Both men responded with a resounding yes. To me, that's all that matters. Somehow, losing her so young feels easier to carry if I know she was truly happy toward the end of her life.

It's common to "try out" a show in a location off the beaten track to work out any kinks in the production. Pittsburgh, Pennsylvania, was chosen for this purpose. Booked into a theater that was a complete dump, according to Walter Painter, the show was received well and gave my mom the confidence she needed to tackle Vegas again. Her performances there in 1968 had been a terrible fiasco, but judging by the response in Pittsburgh, she was much better prepared now.

February of 1974 had my mom returning to Las Vegas for the first time since her ill-fated engagement at Caesars Palace. This time she was to perform at the Flamingo Hilton with comedian Marty Allen. Her show premiered to rave reviews in the local press. The *Las Vegas Sun* wrote, "Cass Elliot, making a strong point that she is no longer Mama Cass, has a good act serving notice that she is here to stay. The audience was with her all the way . . . no empty seats anywhere."

The *Hollywood Reporter* said, "Cass Elliot came ready to take the town by storm, and take it she does with an utterly charming, entertaining and delicious concoction of hit records, old favorites and great gobs of her earthy hit-wit and personality."

Those reviews must have made my mom feel accomplished as a solo act. A career as Cass Elliot, on her own, was finally starting to fall into place.

My mother wasn't the only celebrity performing in Las Vegas that month. Over at the Las Vegas Hilton, Elvis Presley was wrapping up a two-month engagement that ended on February 23, 1974. My mother attended that final show and was invited back to Elvis's suite on the thirtieth floor afterward. Elvis was known for his late-night parties with music and singing into the wee hours. He was partial to singing gospel music, and on this night, he'd invited his former backup group, the Imperials, to join the party. As the evening progressed, my mom was part of the appreciative audience. But something was nagging at her, a question she needed to have answered.

So, she came forward and asked Elvis quite brazenly, "Why do you do this? Why do you sing these same gospel songs over and over again like this?"

"Have you ever tried singing a song with a gospel quartet backing you up?" he asked in return.

She laughed and admitted she never had. Elvis then challenged her to try. After some persuasion, she mustered up the courage to try the only Christian song she knew, "Amazing Grace." She sang it all the way through with the Imperials' beautiful voices backing her up. When she was finished, she turned to Elvis with tears brimming in her eyes. Now she understood, she told him.

After the Vegas run was completed, my mom was booked into the club at the Deauville Hotel in Miami Beach. As the plane was taxiing down the runway for takeoff, she suffered some kind of health incident alarming enough for the pilot to turn the plane around and return everyone to the terminal. Details are sketchy here, and much of what comes next is my speculation. She must have been determined to be stable enough to fly, because she was put onto another flight bound for Los Angeles, where she was hospitalized at Cedars of Lebanon Hospital in Hollywood after landing. Allan Carr initially described her incident to the press as a "seizure of the heart," but later walked the statement back, saying it had been an episode of hypoglycemia. Low blood sugar? It's hard to imagine low blood sugar causing a plane to abandon takeoff, but this is what was reported in the press.

This was the third time my mom had been hospitalized in five months. Hospital records don't exist any longer, in any format. I wish they did, as they could potentially shed light on so much information. I do know that at some point, *possibly* during this February hospitalization, she had her gallbladder removed. I recall being taken to visit her at a hospital in Los Angeles after the operation. It was explained to me that the gallbladder was a part of the body that, over time, our bodies didn't actually need any longer to survive. That being said, my mom didn't need hers anymore, and would be just fine without one. What? How this was explained to a then-six-year-old me is a little mind-boggling. But I understood it as best as a six-year-old could, at the time.

George Caldwell entered the picture in March of 1974, hired by Allan Carr to accompany and assist my mother. Allan must have thought that she'd need someone to watch over her. George became her shadow, and before long my mom developed a crush on him. The relationship with Chris Conroy had apparently run its course, and George stepped right into that role. My mom's friend, actress, model, and author Leon Bing, remembers that my mom had come over to her place, with Caldwell in tow, the day before she was to leave on that last trip abroad. Leon told me that Caldwell gave her very bad vibes the second she laid eyes on him.

Telling my mother that she wanted to show her some new piece of clothing that she'd bought, she brought my mom into the bedroom and closed the door. Leon told my mom she thought George was bad news, that she didn't like him at all. After hearing her out, my mom replied that she was in love with him and was taking him to London. There wasn't anything more that Leon could do or say to deter her. My mom's mind was made up.

I remember my mom telling me that she and George were going to get married when she got home from her trip. She excitedly described the matching long, red velvet dresses we would wear. She must have loved him. I'm not sure if her affections were reciprocated. My mom had a pattern of embellishing relationships until they resembled what she wanted them to be.

On April 26, 1974, I turned seven. A party table was set up for me and my small guests on the long screened porch right off the kitchen in the back of the house. I was sitting there with my friends when my mom swept outside to help sing "Happy Birthday." Afterward, she made a speech wishing me a happy birthday and added an additional bit of information at the end about how seven was a lucky number. I believed her at that moment, but I soon learned not to be sold on the Lucky Seven thing.

My mom made her final appearance on *The Tonight Show* on May 7, 1974. Greeting her, Johnny made a comment about the show being a sort of "jinx" for her. Back in the beginning of April, she'd been booked as a guest. Her appearance that day had ended in a disaster. Soon after her arrival at NBC Studios in Burbank, she had tripped on a section of uneven pavement and been rushed to a nearby hospital for assessment.

That was hospitalization number four in a seven-month period.

Needless to say, she hadn't been on the show *that* night. She'd been rebooked for later that month, April 23. That time, she'd been in her dressing room getting ready and became lightheaded and dizzy before she lost consciousness. She'd again been taken to a nearby hospital—hospitalization number *five*, this time on a stretcher. Pictures were snapped, and the event made the national news.

Recounting the series of ordeals to Johnny, she chalked up that last incident to having "the vapors," just like Blanche DuBois in *A Streetcar Named Desire*.

"I had a very bad headache that day, and I hadn't been able to eat anything all day. Ordinarily, you wouldn't think that would have been such a hardship for me," she said as the audience tittered. "But my blood sugar level dropped or something and I just sort of tipped over." She gestured a tipping motion with her hands. "I spent about four days in the hospital, and please . . . I got so many nice cards from folks and everything, but I was on the *news*"—she paused to sigh—"which is really grim because my mother didn't know about it, and she saw it on the news."

"Scares people to death," Johnny remarked.

"Then I had some friends of mine in Paris that called. It made the papers in Paris. I mean, I could work ALL my life and do something really good, a good piece of work, and nobody would ever hear about it. And just tip over somewhere where there's a camera, and . . ." she made a clicking sound as if she were a photographer snapping quick shots. The rabid paparazzi type of photographer was just beginning to be a thing.

Again, something seems like it was happening healthwise with my mom. Five hospitalizations in seven months? I can't imagine how this was not being noticed by her management and the people around her. The only possible explanation I can come up with is so ugly at its core that I hate to even think about it. Could people have been looking the other way, naively hoping for the best, with the tour in Europe happening so soon? With so much riding on getting her to London, both financially and professionally for my mom and others, were they willfully turning a blind eye?

As the summer approached and the European tour loomed, a few loose ends needed to be tied up by my mom's business managers: airfare and hotel costs for everyone involved in the show had to be arranged, and musicians needed to be hired and paid for. These costs were typically borne by the artist in the hope that the shows would turn a profit. To cover these enormous upfront costs, my mom's business managers relied on their relationship with a prominent bank to get her approved for unsecured personal loans.

In a different form of preparation, my mom began a bit of physical exercise, joining the Hollywood Tennis Club. I would go with her and watch her run around on the court, pretending it was my job to chase all the stray tennis balls when they bounced out of range. We spent a lot of time together in those weeks before she left for London, and I flew to Baltimore to stay with Grandma Bess. Her tour would last for a few weeks, so it made sense for me to spend time with Grandma and get to just be a kid for the summer.

That fall I would be starting second grade in a new school, and I was excited and nervous about it. Oakwood School, a private K–12 school in North Hollywood, had seemed like a nice place when we visited the campus that spring. I'd gone to visit a classroom, while my mom visited with the school administration. The kids seemed to be having a good time there. My mother was scheduled to return from Europe just before the school year started, and she'd be there to hear all about my first day. That was the plan, anyway.

Except she never made it home. And I would be left to start the second grade, and everything that came after, without her.

CHAPTER 11

AUGUST 2, 1974, WAS SEASONABLY HOT IN LOS ANGE-
les, nearly ninety degrees. Getting dressed for my mother's funeral that morning, I felt awkward in the white dress
with green stripes and a matching coat that had been purchased for me. I also had new, stiff white shoes to wear. I felt
weird being dressed so brightly in white. Even at that young
age, I knew somewhere that black was for funerals and white
was for weddings. I felt that I should have been wearing black
or *something* sadder than the white suit I'd been given.

The services were held at Hollywood Memorial Park, on
the Paramount Pictures Studios lot. More than 400 people
were in attendance. Photographers seemed to be everywhere,
crowded in tight clusters in front of the limos, sticking their
huge lenses inside the open windows to nail their shots. So
many friends and colleagues of my mother turned out to
pay tribute to her: actors Peter Lawford and Jack Nicholson;
producer Lou Adler; John Phillips and his wife, model and

actress Genevieve Waite; Michelle Phillips; fellow musicians like Sonny Bono, and of course, her old friend Denny Doherty. With the same intensity she'd been loved by her friends during her life, so too was she mourned by them after her death.

Just four days ago I'd been sitting in Grandma Bess's house in Baltimore, listening to the impossible news that my mother had died in London. I was having a hard time believing the "permanent" part of it all. Yet here we were at a funeral in her honor, with her body lying inside a big white box.

Our family was seated in a section behind a curtain allowing for a degree of privacy for us as we grieved. Sliding into the seat next to Grandma Bess, Denny said simply and softly to her, "I'm sorry for your loss, ma'am." There wasn't much else to really say at a time like that, and his minimalist and heartfelt choice of words likely touched my grandmother deeply.

When the time came for our family to walk by my mother's casket, my uncle Russ, Leah's husband, picked me up and held me close as we slowly passed by the closed, long white box that I knew somehow contained my mom. I would learn later why the casket was closed. In Judaism, it's the custom, because bodies are not embalmed and remain in their natural state. I wondered *where* exactly she was in there, where was her head and where were her feet? It felt very real, very scary, and at the same time, totally unreal.

What does a seven-year-old understand about death? As it turns out, not much. I do remember being confused and just following along, doing what I was told to do. I'm not sure that

I fully grasped what was happening. Part of me still thought my mom wasn't really dead, whatever that meant to little me. Many years later, in therapy, I learned something significant that helped me to understand this confusion. My therapist told me that the idea of death, the very *concept* of it, is impossible for young children to understand. So much so that even the death of a family pet may be very hard for a little one to wrap their still developing brain around.

Looking back, I feel such empathy for myself at that age. My entire life had just changed, and was going to change much more, and I really had no idea what was happening to me.

Then, just like that, the funeral was abruptly over.

We stood up and walked out as a family, first Grandma Bess with Bubby and Ben and her sister, Lily, followed by a group of cousins, and finally my aunt Leah and uncle Russ, still carrying me. Grandma Bess headed toward one limo, whereas Leah and Russ and Uncle Joe were destined for another.

"Who do you want to ride with?"

I don't remember who asked me this question, but I remember the rest of that moment in vivid detail.

Who do you want to ride with? The choice, I understood, was between Grandma Bess or Leah and Russ.

There were only two options, and I had to choose one. The decision felt heavy, like a weight. Almost fifty years later, I can still feel that child inside me, being asked to make an almost impossible choice, although back then I couldn't possibly have known how important that choice would be.

I wanted to be in the car with Grandma Bess. That much I knew. I loved her so much. But by this point I had been told that I would be going to live with Leah, Russ, and their son Nathaniel. This way, I would have as close to a nuclear family situation as possible.

Leah and Russ had recently purchased a home not far from our house in the Hollywood Hills, and the idea of living with them didn't feel entirely foreign to me. Knowing that this was going to be my new setup, I thought to myself that I'd better start getting used to my new life, and the sooner the better. So, I chose Leah and Russ.

When I think about the sheer gravity of that decision, I feel all the feelings. Sad for that little girl. Angry that I had to make that choice. And also, the mashup of feelings from back then: Lonely. Confused. Scared. With my mother gone, I felt as if I were now on my own. Having to face grown-up situations at seven will do that to you.

Because it was oppressively hot the day of the funeral, the limo drivers were waiting for us in shady spots under a row of nearby trees. To keep the interiors of the black cars cool and comfortable, they'd opened all the windows. When the service ended abruptly, the limos were still parked under the trees with the windows down when we climbed into the back. That meant we were like sitting ducks for the photographers' long lenses pointed directly in our faces.

One of the pictures taken that day continues to haunt me. There we are, sitting in the back seat of the limo: Uncle Joe,

Leah, and Russ, with me on his lap. Shock and sorrow are apparent in everyone's eyes. In one of the many shots taken that day, I'm looking directly at the camera, and I look devastated, all of our individual and collective pain captured and frozen in time.

In the weeks that followed, and in fact for many months afterward, I would console myself at night before I'd drift into sleep with the thought that all of the adults around me were wrong. *My mom is just on the road working like always,* I told myself. *She'll be coming back soon. She has to. Because I'm here, and I know she would never leave me.*

As we drove out of the cemetery that day, unbeknownst to any of us, a six-foot-three, left-handed guitar player stood across the street quietly weeping, unable to bring himself to walk across the road to pay tribute to the mother of his child. My mother had kept his identity a secret for more than seven years. He'd met me just once, with the specific understanding that he would not say he was my father, and he'd complied. I wouldn't meet him again until I was twenty, when he told me that he'd been at the funeral that day. I was instantly angry, but I also couldn't help seeing the irony—that he hadn't been man enough to cross the street and mourn the passing of the woman he'd officially made into a mama.

CHAPTER 12

ALMOST IMMEDIATELY AFTER THE FUNERAL, LEAH brought me to Martha's Vineyard, where she and Nathaniel had been vacationing when she received the news that her sister had died. She'd left Nathaniel in the care of friends and needed to bring him back home.

Before flying back to LA, we spent some time with Leah's friends Arlo and Jackie Guthrie at their farm in the Berkshires. Leah and Arlo had been friends since the Stockbridge School, where they'd met. The Stockbridge School was the boarding school in Massachusetts that Leah had attended, and they'd stayed in touch.

In the Berkshires, Nathaniel and I played outside every day. He was almost four by now, and fun to play with. Leah brought us for rides on country roads, and one afternoon, we stumbled upon an old farmhouse for sale. It was in Middlefield, a few towns over from where we were staying, and owned by a sweet old couple named the Gardners. Mr. Gardner had been born and raised in Middlefield and had lived in nearly every house in the town, which was a true one-road-in/one-road-out sort of place. The center of Middlefield had a general store, which doubled as the US Post Office, and also featured the town's only gas pump. The church also functioned as the town hall. To say this was a small town is an understatement.

Leah and Russ bought the old farmhouse and its surrounding hundred acres from the aging Gardners, who had already built themselves a new, smaller house across the road. They would be our neighbors, and lived there until they passed away many years later.

After my mother died, her lawyers weren't able to locate a will. According to California law, that meant her estate was considered "intestate." As such, all assets were to pass on to her closest living relative which, in this case, was seven-year-old me.

Grandma Bess was appointed executor of my mom's estate, which was in deplorable shape. Her bank accounts were empty. Her business managers had, by powers granted by my mother, been paying her bills every month without fail. There were additional worries, mostly pertaining to the multiple unsecured personal loans that had been taken out to cover the huge costs of the London shows. Now those loans were due in full, and although the powers that my mother assigned to her business managers expired upon her death, loan repayment checks were backdated, and her bank accounts cleaned out. They had cosigned for those loans and didn't want to be liable for them.

In effect, they saved their own asses and left their client's family with nothing in the bank.

Basically, we were broke. And still, bills were coming in. Without any liquid assets to draw from, and with a growing mountain of debt, the family had few options. The estate lawyers from Mitchell, Silberberg and Knupp advised Grandma Bess to sell the house. There was no other way to make ends meet.

And so, our house on Woodrow Wilson, my mother's Hollywood Hills sanctuary, the site of so many legendary musical gatherings, the only place I'd ever called home, was put up for sale. It was purchased by a doctor, if I remember correctly, who sold it a few years later to Harry Nilsson, who rented it to Beatle Ringo Starr.

After the house had been sold, one of the lawyers from Mitchell, Silberberg and Knupp approached Grandma Bess at a procedural estate hearing in court. He needed to inform her, he said, that the firm had a conflict of interest with the estate. They also represented the bank that held the mortgage and had also funded the outstanding personal loans. Had the law firm pressed for the sale of my mother's house to appease their other client? There had been no other option to pay the estate's bills other than to sell the house, but still, my grandma fired the law firm on the spot.

—■—

Though my mom had chosen the progressive Oakwood School for me and enrolled me in second grade there before she died, my tuition had not been paid. It was already almost fall and I needed to go to school somewhere, so I was enrolled at Valley View Elementary, the local public elementary school in the Hollywood Hills near Leah and Russ's house. During my first few days there, the administration decided my reading and writing skills were too advanced for the second grade and bumped me up a grade. But after a week or so, it was clear I wasn't emotionally ready for third grade. So back to the second grade I went. I may have been good at reading and spelling, but I was understandably traumatized. My entire world had been turned upside down just one month earlier, and I was trying to figure out which end was up.

I'd been living with Leah and Russ for about six months when Leah became aware of certain idiosyncrasies in my behavior. She would hear noises in the middle of the night, and follow them to discover that it was me, making my way to the bathroom. She would find me sitting on the toilet, fast asleep, with my thumb in my mouth. I'd trained myself to wake up multiple times at night to use the bathroom. My nanny Virginia had made her mark with that wooden spoon when potty training me.

Leah also noticed that I had trouble catching a ball and was lacking in some other basic motor skills. She reached out to a friend of hers who was studying child psychiatry for advice. He recommended that I see one of his professors who had a private practice in Beverly Hills. But before I met with him,

Leah spoke with him a few times to tell him about me and my story.

Before Dr. Yahalom agreed to treat me, he told Leah that he wanted to put me through some tests at the Reiss-Davis Child Study Institute. Though I scored very high on the intelligence portion, I scored extremely low on the developmental scale. These severe discrepancies indicated that I had suffered some sort of trauma, the psychiatrist told Leah. He also reported that I was confused about certain things. For instance, he told Leah that I had no concept of what a "daddy" did. But thinking about it now, how could I have known this when I'd never had one? With no example to refer to, no frame of reference, I didn't even know I was missing anything.

Dr. Yahalom was a middle-aged grandfatherly type with a thick Israeli accent. He was warm, friendly, and comforting and wore sweater vests under his sport coats. Once a week, for the next three years, I went to his office in the heart of Beverly Hills. It was located in one of the medical office buildings on Bedford Drive. When I opened the door from the hallway to the main outer office I'd be greeted by low lighting and stillness. The windows in the inner office, where we had our sessions, faced the rear alley, offering a view of a splendid brick wall. I'd barely get the outer door open and closed before Dr. Yahalom would appear to greet me and usher me into the inner office space.

Once inside, I knew the routine.

First, check the small refrigerator in his office. There were always chilled Reese's peanut butter cups inside. Always. I would grab some candy and sit down, unwrapping each one carefully. Dr. Yahalom would then gently prod me to tell him what was happening in my young life and patiently draw out my answers. He had lots of toys in his office, and I'd play with them as he watched and asked me questions. Before long, I figured out how to work this situation to my advantage. I realized that if I had a desire for any new toy that I'd seen, all I needed to do was mention it in a session, and it would be there at my next appointment.

I had weekly visits with Dr. Yahalom until I was around ten. Every week, I would be picked up early from school, usually by Leah, and driven to Beverly Hills to my appointment. I put two and two together and decided I was seeing him to try to feel better about losing my mom. That's how my mind was working at the time: I was trying to make sense of my world, which no longer made much sense to me. Seeing Dr. Yahalom on a regular basis was something I could count on happening every single week, and there were always those cold Reese's peanut butter cups to count on. And in my life so far, there hadn't been many things that I could always count on. Maybe that was the point of the peanut butter cups, to teach me that in some small way that I could count on something, no matter how small.

Having Dr. Yahalom to talk with every week gave me a kind of stability I'd never known before, and slowly, I started to trust and talk with him. Many, many times as an adult, I have reflected on my time spent with him and been flooded with gratitude. I only wish that I had been able to tell him how much he helped me, but I wasn't. By the time I reached that point in maturity, he had long since passed away.

When my second-grade year was complete, Russ headed out on the road with James Taylor for the summer and Leah, Nathaniel, and I headed to the farm in Middlefield, which would become our summer retreat from Los Angeles. Russ was always on tour with a band in the summers, and Leah, Nathaniel, and I would pack up and leave LA when the school year ended and return before it began again in the fall. We would spend the days outside, wandering around on the property picking wild blueberries until our bellies ached. And on hot, muggy summer afternoons, just as the heat would seem extra hot and heavy, the dark clouds would build. Summer electrical storms would bring lightning and thunder the likes of which I had never experienced as a California girl. Sure, we had the occasional thunderstorm in LA, but these were nothing in comparison to the summer storms in western Massachusetts. These were truly next-level and would leave almost as quickly as they had come on.

Nathaniel and I both loved playing with our miniature toy Corgi cars underneath the old elm tree in front of the house in Middlefield. Corgis were little die-cast replicas of actual vehicles, like James Bond's car, that were made in the UK. In 1977 the company released a replica of the Queen's Rolls-Royce with doors that actually opened. That was my favorite Corgi. Russ would search for Corgi cars when he was traveling on the road and bring Nathaniel and me each a gift of one when he came home. We'd make roads and little towns to drive our toy cars around. We'd imagine the people in our little towns going about their days, going to the grocery store and to the post office running their errands.

When we returned to LA in that fall of 1975, Nathaniel and I both started school in Hollywood, at the Founder's School at Temple Israel. He was in kindergarten, and I was in the third grade. Around this time, I was becoming more aware of my family situation, including my last name. Legally, my name was Owen Vanessa Hendricks, which was just one of many things that didn't make sense to me. Why was my last name different from my mother's and, more importantly, from this new family's, if I was really part of their family now? Didn't my last name need to be the same as theirs for me to truly belong?

I asked Leah about this on the way to school one morning. When she and Russ had decided to raise me, she explained, they had talked about changing my last name but had decided that Owen Hendricks sounded better than Owen Kunkel. That Owen Hendricks sounded more "rock and roll," she chuckled. In the same breath, she assured me that having a different last name in no way meant that I wasn't part of the family. Years later, I found one of my old Pee Chee schoolwork folders, with my name written in my childlike scrawl at the top: "Owen

Kunkel." I wanted to feel as if I was truly a part of my new family, and to me that meant having the same last name.

In 1976 we drove across the country to Middlefield instead of flying, all four of us—Russ, Leah, Nathaniel, and me—packed into an orange International Scout II four-wheel-drive truck. The Scout was what we would now refer to as an SUV. Russ had the rear seat removed from the vehicle and a custom-made platform constructed for the entire back section. He had a mattress made to fit over the platform, covered with brown corduroy. This was for Nathaniel and me to have a place to lie down and relax the whole way across the country with our puppy, Lupe.

We had adopted Lupe from friends of the family, whose two dogs had a litter of puppies. Lupe's mom was a malamute husky, and her dad was a big black Newfoundland aptly named Eclipse. Lupe was beautiful. She had the fur of a malamute that made her look more like her mom than her dad. Along with Lupe we also had Chocolate, an Irish water spaniel, with brown curls in her coat and the long ears of a spaniel. Sweetest dog ever, Chocolate was. I adored her. Years later I had a blonde cocker spaniel that I named Nilla, as in Vanilla, as a nod to the memory of Chocolate.

Our luggage was stored comfortably under the mattress platform in the back. Russ had also replaced the car's factory-issued front seats with more comfortable captain's seats, and he'd installed a CB radio so we could listen to the truck drivers along the highways as we traveled east. That trip was long. I remember very little besides looking out the window at the road in front of us, which seemed utterly endless. At one motel where we stopped along the way, we left Lupe in the Scout overnight when we went inside to sleep. When we got up the following morning, we discovered she had been less than pleased to have been left alone and had chewed the armrests of the new captain's seats down to nubs of what they had been before. Lupe slept inside with us every night for the remainder of the trip, and I'm pretty sure Russ never fully forgave that dog for disrespecting the seats like that.

The summer of 1976, July 4 was the United States Bicentennial, and we celebrated the holiday at the Middlefield Fair. I had also received a box from Aunt Lil, sent to me in Middlefield. The box was heavy and contained lots of old books. There were complete sets of a few different series. There was the Nancy Drew series, and the Hardy Boys as well. Also in the collection were a couple of new series to me, the Dana Girls and the Bobbsey Twins. The books were all obviously from many decades before my time, and I loved reading all of them. And when I'd read them, every now and again as I turned the pages, sometimes a pressed rose petal would fall into my lap. When it happened, I was always reminded that someone had read this book before me and thought it a good place to keep what was obviously a special rose.

Lupe was literally in paradise from the moment she arrived in Middlefield with us, scampering around the farm every day without having to be on a leash or contained in any way. Having her freedom agreed with Lupe so much that at the end of that summer it was decided that she would stay in Massachusetts after we closed up the farmhouse and returned to LA. The sweet neighbors we'd bought the farm from, the Gardners, agreed to keep Lupe there. They loved that dog. That way we could visit her when we came for our annual visit to Middlefield. Which we did, every summer for the next five years.

At the beginning of my fifth-grade year, Nathaniel and I were enrolled at Oakwood School, the same school I was supposed to attend just three years earlier, before my mom died. It made me happy to know I was going to a school my mom had chosen for me, even if she wasn't here anymore. I slowly started to make new friends at Oakwood. Life started to take on a "new normal" shape. It wasn't the life I'd known before, but it was one I began to settle into—stable and predictable, which was what I craved after so much upheaval.

Oakwood in the seventies was vastly smaller than it is today, with one class per grade of no more than twenty-five students. Lots of kids who had parents who worked in entertainment went to Oakwood. Some were in the music business; some were actors. We all knew each other on some level, which contributed to the feeling of an intimate school community that

Oakwood enjoyed. The school followed a progressive curriculum, and we learned all sorts of cool things there beyond the expected reading and math. I loved the elective classes, which combined grade levels together according to interests from woodworking to calligraphy. Kids could take an extra art class, perhaps a pottery class, or—as I chose—the music and theater elective.

In chorus class, we sang current hits like "Bohemian Rhapsody" by Queen. In theater class, the students also put on a performance at the end of every semester to show what they'd learned. We were putting on a performance of the popular children's record, *Free to Be . . . You and Me* by Marlo Thomas. It was the first time I'd ever been involved in any sort of play. We were all assigned parts of the songs to learn, with corresponding scenes that we planned around the songs. I was chosen to sing "When I Grow Up" with a girl named Jamie Green and another girl named Wendy Wilson. Wendy was in Nathaniel's class, and had an older sister named Carnie. Carnie was one grade below me, and we all knew each other already because we had been in a school carpool for a while together. Carnie and Wendy's father was one of the Beach Boys, Brian Wilson. Carnie and Wendy would both become very dear friends to me at pivotal times in my life, and we'd even sing together as adults.

I had stayed in touch with my friend Misty, who'd lived in the house just up the road from me and my mom in the Hollywood Hills. Misty and I still spent almost every weekend together, trading off sleepover locations from weekend to weekend. To walk to Misty's house, I'd have to pass our old house on Woodrow Wilson, and more than once I'd imagine my mother running out onto the driveway to meet me, as if she'd been waiting for me and the past few years had all been some big joke.

At Misty's house we would swim in her pool, play with Barbie dolls, and swing on the swingset for hours. We'd never want our weekends to end and to have to separate. One of us would nominate the other to call the parent who was coming to pick up the departing friend. "I called last time; you have to call this time!" We'd beg for an hour more, maybe just half an hour? Sometimes we'd get more time, and sometimes we wouldn't, but we were always up for the challenge. And when we'd get our way we'd face each other, put our hands on each other's shoulders, and start bouncing up and down and whooping with excitement.

One Wednesday afternoon in late November 1979, I was coming home from school in my carpool. As we drove home along Mulholland Drive, I looked out the window, like I always did, at the houses on the hilltop where my old house with my mom had been. I could usually see a window or two of the house from Mulholland, but that day was different. That day I saw thick black smoke rising from that area. I instantly knew it was coming from the old house. I could just feel it. Later that night my feeling was confirmed on the news. Ringo Starr, the house's current occupant, had been making a fire in the fireplace on that cold November afternoon when a spark from the chimney, it was believed, set the second floor on fire. There he was on the news talking to reporters, as neighbor Chevy Chase walked around in the background inspecting things.

The following weekend, I was at Misty's house, and she and I decided to go down to the old house and investigate for ourselves. When we got there, we could see the house was burned on the top portion, and on some of the lower parts as well. It didn't look like my house anymore. Where my mom's room and my room had been were totally gone. The lot smelled faintly of smoke, and piles of burned and melted record albums and 45 singles littered the front yard, some of them having the Beatles' name on them. I do recall feeling badly for Ringo, who had so obviously lost things that were special to him in that fire. I didn't realize until much later that Ringo did indeed lose hundreds of items from his personal Beatles memorabilia collection that day.

Russ was working constantly and wasn't around a whole lot back then. He was now a well-known rock drummer, performing with Jackson Browne, James Taylor, Carole King, and other well-known stars in the 1970s. In those days, musicians would work on the recording of an artist's new album and then be tapped to accompany the artist on the road when they toured to support the album. Many times, the same group of musicians would be hired together to work with different artists. Before long, these musicians earned themselves the respect and admiration of their peers. Many of these musicians are still working to this day.

Leah had also continued to follow her passion of being a singer-songwriter and had been performing around the LA club scene with friends like Stephen Bishop. She landed a recording contract with Columbia Records in 1978 and began working on her first solo studio album. At night, after Nathaniel and I were in bed, Leah would go downstairs to the piano and play her songs.

I can't even estimate how many nights we fell asleep to the sound of her singing and playing the piano. There were that many. My memories of those nights remain some of my fondest in recollection of those years. I felt safe and warm in my bed on those nights, with my bedroom door a little bit ajar, just the way I liked it to be.

On other nights, I'd stay up reading. I loved to read and would get so involved in the story I was reading that I'd find it impossible to put the book down and go to sleep. Leah would frequently have to remind me to shut my light off and go to bed. I was a big Judy Blume fan, and also liked the requisite preteen romance novels as well.

I finished both fifth and sixth grade at Lower Oakwood and matriculated to the upper school campus in 1979. Classes were different now that I was in the seventh grade. There was more homework, and I found it hard to keep my grades up at an acceptable level. I remember struggling to pay attention and forgetting to write down homework assignments. On the first day of class, it was customary to go around the circle and let students introduce themselves. On the first day of seventh grade, we went around the circle in music class, and I told everyone my name and added that I had been born and raised on an Israeli kibbutz.

A couple of hours after I got home from school that day, Leah knocked on my bedroom door. She'd just gotten a call from the music teacher, who had informed her of my "great story." I was developing a talent for telling tall tales. I'd just done it for attention.

Being at the upper school also meant that our class got much bigger. At the middle school, our class went from a class of twenty-five students to a class of nearly seventy-five. We got a lot of new students, and we all began to get to know one another. The school sent an official roster home with each student to facilitate get-togethers for the students. There were a few new girls that I'd begun to hang out with a little bit at lunchtime and at recess. There was a new girl named Shannon Ahern who was from Canada, a girl from New York named Jenny Masser, and a girl named Moon Zappa, who lived on Woodrow Wilson Drive, near my old house. All three girls' dads were in the music business in different capacities. Jenny's dad, Michael Masser, was a successful songwriter, having penned the hit "The Greatest Love of All." Moon's dad was Frank Zappa of Frank Zappa and The Mothers of Invention, and Shannon's dad, Brian Ahern, was a well-known record producer who was currently married to country music star Emmylou Harris. Shannon and I hit it off immediately. One weekend, I decided to give her a call to make plans.

Finding her name in the school roster, I dialed the number listed on the page. The phone rang, and soon a woman's voice picked up. I asked politely if Shannon was home. She wasn't, and the woman asked my name, so that she could tell Shannon who'd called for her. "Owen Hendricks," I replied, as she wrote down my name.

When Shannon called me back later that day, she had some very interesting news. The lady who had answered the phone when I'd called had been her stepmother Emmylou's costume designer, Vanessa. Vanessa Hendricks was her name, and she indeed was the very same Vanessa Hendricks who had been married to Jim Hendricks all those years ago. The same Vanessa I'd been named for, she'd told Shannon excitedly that day, when she realized that I was *that* Owen Hendricks. She'd even told her that she was my godmother. Vanessa was excited to have made contact with me, and we stayed in touch for a long while after that.

CHAPTER 13

EIGHTH GRADE WAS A CHALLENGE FOR ME. I WAS not doing well academically, at all. I had been finding it harder and harder to pay attention to my teachers. As they lectured, I would look out the window and let myself float away, lost in my own thoughts. I'd have to force myself to concentrate on my classwork, which was often not completed. Teachers would consistently comment on my report cards about the potential I had, if I could just be more focused and organized. I found this to be next to impossible to accomplish. Today, I'd likely be labeled ADHD, but in reality, I was "only" traumatized.

Leah and Russ also separated around this time, and Russ moved out. If I'm honest, it didn't feel as if our home life had changed in a big way. He hadn't been home that much anyway. I didn't see a lot of Russ for a while after that. His visits were mostly with Nathaniel, and for the first time it became clear to me that Russ wasn't really my dad. At least it didn't seem that way now, because it didn't feel like he was making much of an effort to spend time with me.

Leah was working a lot, traveling and performing in support of her records. Her second album had recently been released. She'd also contributed backup vocals on James Taylor's 1977 hit "Handyman" and been responsible for the unmistakable background parts of "Come on, come on, come on, come on." Leah, like her sister, has a singing voice that is instantly recognizable the minute you hear her. That Cohen Honk at its finest.

Although we didn't spend a lot of time together after my mom died, John and Michelle Phillips's daughter Chynna and I were still frequent guests at each other's birthday parties. In February 1978, Chynna turned ten and was having a party at a nightclub in Hollywood on Sunset Boulevard called the Roxy. The Roxy was one of the nightclub properties that was owned or partially owned by the former producer of the Mamas and the Papas, Lou Adler. Michelle had remained close with him over the years. Actually, the party was upstairs at the private club called On the Rox, where we all gathered together, danced, and laughed. The floor vibrated with the sound of the band playing loudly below us, a band called Toto. They had a current hit single called "Hold the Line" that was all over the radio stations at the time. They started to play it that night, and we could hear it upstairs. I really liked that song; it was definitely one of my favorites. I dropped to the floor and put my ear directly on the ground to hear it better. I'll never forget it.

——■——

After a long period of stability, big changes were happening for our family again. Leah decided that the best decision for her, Nathaniel, and me would be to leave Los Angeles and move to Massachusetts. Los Angeles in the late 1970s was a difficult place to raise kids, and there were not a lot of safe places for kids to hang out. Leah found a house in Northampton, Massachusetts, about an hour from the farm where we'd spent so many summers. Northampton, a town of about 30,000 people, would offer us a new life, in a place surrounded by universities and culture, where we didn't have to go to private school to get a decent education. We would be moving at the end of the school year. But until then, Leah had a lot of work scheduled. When the option for me to live with Grandma Bess for the rest of my eighth-grade year was offered, it took me less than a hot minute to say yes.

Living with Grandma sounded like heaven to me. After my mom passed away, Grandma had returned to Baltimore only briefly before moving to LA to be closer to the rest of us. She'd officially transferred from the Baltimore office of Social Security, where she'd worked for years, to the Social Security office in Canoga Park. Before long, she purchased a townhouse in an area of the San Fernando Valley that she loved.

Her work ethic was extraordinary, though not surprising for a Cohen. She would wake at five-thirty—as she had in the food truck days—and be at work by eight a.m., five days a week. Work ended at four-thirty p.m., and she'd usually get home around five. If the Dodgers were playing a night game, nothing else was happening as far as she was concerned. The radio or TV would stay on through dinner and the dishes, turned off only for the time it took her to get upstairs to her room and flip the game on there. The way my mother had loved football, my grandmother loved baseball with a passion, even taking me to my very first baseball game the fateful summer my mom died to watch her beloved Orioles play at historic Camden Yards.

Now I would stay with Grandma all the time, not just on weekends like Nathaniel and I sometimes did. The only hiccup was figuring out how I would get to and from school. Grandma left for work before I was even awake, and my school day ended before her workday did. The answer was to hire a taxi service to pick me up in the morning and bring me home in the afternoon.

After I finished the eighth grade, we made the move to Massachusetts. The house Leah had found in Northampton had been built in the 1700s, and the ceilings and doorways were much lower than any I'd encountered before. I was told humans had been smaller when the house was built, which sounded unbelievable. But the house itself was cozy and welcoming, in spite of its immense size.

The town of Northampton was settled before the Revolutionary War and is rich in history. Notably, Calvin Coolidge, the thirtieth president of the United States, who had been an attorney and Republican politician, spent the latter part of his life there until he passed away in 1933. In honor of Coolidge, there are various homages to him in town, including the bridge across the Connecticut River that's named for him. Northampton's Forbes Library, just outside the gates of renowned women's school Smith College, has a dedicated room known as the Presidential Library for President Coolidge. We arrived during the summer months and began exploring this part of Massachusetts, getting to know our new hometown before school began in the fall. Leah suggested I volunteer at the local hospital as a candy striper, where I delivered floral arrangements to the patients.

I started the ninth grade at Northampton High School in September of 1981. Northampton High seemed to be straight out of one of the Harlequin romance novels I had been voraciously reading. The building was constructed in 1899 and had long hallways with shiny floors and student lockers lining the walls. The feeling of days gone by and all the students that had walked the halls before me was palpable.

I was still dressing as if I were living in Los Angeles, with my army-green parachute pants and my green-silver ballet flats. Some kids thought I was weird, which of course was and is true, but there were a few who took a chance and befriended me. After all, I was from LOS ANGELES, and my parents were DIVORCED, were the whispers my friends later confessed to me. Before long, I found my people. They called themselves "Techies" and spent all of their extra time before and after school hanging out in the backstage area of the school auditorium. The theater people. Of *course* I'd feel the most at ease there with creative-minded types. The Techies embraced me as the newcomer, and I felt immediately at home.

I also started to make friends with kids in my classes, even though for a little while I was definitely sticking out like a sore thumb. We got in the bad habit of leaving school during the day during free period. Donna lived four houses or so down on Elm Street, and we'd sneak over there to eat Cap'n Crunch cereal and watch *General Hospital.* There was a show that came on after the soap opera with a lady named Oprah that we liked, too. Sometimes we'd make it back to school for the last class of the day, but not often. It wouldn't be a big stretch here to say that school was still not my thing.

In the Northampton High theater program, the Techies were responsible for building the sets and running backstage operations for all school performances and plays. Every year, the department produced a spring musical. The year I arrived in Northampton the musical was to be *George M!,* about the life of legendary Broadway singer and songwriter George

M. Cohan. Cohan had penned songs like "Give My Regards to Broadway," "You're a Grand Old Flag," and "I'm a Yankee Doodle Dandy."

Landing a part in the musical would give me the perfect excuse to be hanging around the stage for all the extra hours that would be required for rehearsals, and I decided to audition. We were all getting used to our new lives in a new place, and adjusting wasn't always easy. I missed LA, and my friends there, especially Misty. We wrote letters back and forth regularly and talked by phone as best we could, but it just wasn't the same as being able to walk to her house every weekend.

When the parts were announced, I'd been cast in the chorus and also given a two-line solo to sing. I was the only ninth grader to land a solo, and I was nervous but excited. As nerve-racking as it was to stand on a stage in front of an auditorium full of strangers, I loved performing. *Really* loved it. Just as my mom had gotten her start on stage, the Northampton High School stage was where the showbiz bug nipped at me for the first time. It would soon become a relentless companion, like a stuffy nose that just won't go away.

As the end of the ninth grade approached, my report card was far less than satisfactory. With all of the skipped classes, I was barely passing. How much did I care about this at the time? Not much. I was emerging as a rebellious teenager, and Leah must have been at her wit's end with me. I know I would have been, had the situation been reversed by some strange turn of the universe. At some point around then, a friend of

Leah's recommended a boarding school that had a reputation for straightening kids out. She suggested the idea to me, and I was eager to check it out, so we drove up to have an interview and a tour.

The DeSisto School in Stockbridge, by sheer coincidence, was located on the campus of what had formerly been the Stockbridge School, the very same school that Leah had attended for her eleventh-grade year. This school was different from an ordinary boarding school in that it was a "therapeutic" environment. Everyone had weekly sessions with an assigned therapist on campus.

The DeSisto School was spread out over a large and beautiful campus, the centerpiece of which was known as the Mansion. And a mansion it was indeed. Originally built in 1892, it was known as one of the Berkshire Cottages of the Gilded Age. Large enough to not only house the offices of the school administration, it also had two areas upstairs that were divided into two dormitories. There was also a gymnasium, a large dining hall, a classroom building, and three additional two-story dormitory buildings. When I went on the tour with one of the students, I noticed that everyone seemed to be close friends and were even holding hands as they walked around the campus together. This looked great to me and was part of what made me excited to start at the new school next fall. I would later learn that the handholding wasn't because the students liked each other; it was a tool used to keep people physically close to one another. The school called it "leashing," as in dog leashing.

Summer would come first, and I had been chosen for a summer theater program at Mount Holyoke College that I'd auditioned for back in the spring. Mount Holyoke, just a few towns over from Northampton, is one of the Seven Sisters consortium of colleges that include Vassar, Smith, Bryn Mawr, Wellesley, Radcliffe, and Barnard. The campus has over twenty dormitories, and in the summer the students weren't on campus, so the summer program was able to take over. We'd live there all summer. Good practice, I thought, for going away officially to school in just a few short months.

Each month when Leah would get the telephone bill, I'd have the riot act read to me over the long-distance charges I'd incurred calling California to talk to Misty. Now she was going to come to visit me in Northampton right after her school ended that June. Maybe the grownups figured that buying a plane ticket would be cheaper than all those long-distance telephone calls, so Misty came to stay with us for a little while. It was so great having her there. She came to school with me and met my new friends. The days flew by, and before long, her trip was nearly over. We couldn't bear the idea of separating again. Leah made a few phone calls and spoke with Misty's parents and with the Mount Holyoke College summer theater program. There was space for an extra student, and with her parents' blessing, Misty stayed for the whole summer.

We were elated beyond belief. Soon Misty and I moved into our dorm room together at the college. We were theater apprentices, which meant we helped to build sets for the plays that were put on by college-aged students every two weeks. We had an absolute blast, until Misty contracted the chicken pox virus, from G-d knows who, and two weeks later, I got it too. Hell of a way to end the summer, but that's what happened. Itchy.

After the program ended, Misty and I said goodbye. She went home to Los Angeles, and I got ready to go to boarding school. To me, the idea of boarding school meant argyle sweaters and penny loafers, both of which I had at the ready. I'd slipped dimes into the front of my "penny" loafers, considering inflation, and I was all set to go. Little did I know what I was really getting into, but I'd find out before long.

DeSisto School had been started in 1978 by a man named Michael DeSisto, who had previously been director of a school called the Lake Grove School on Long Island. After being fired from that position, he managed to convince around a third of the faculty and student body to leave with him. Raising $180,000 in advance tuition fees, he purchased the old Stockbridge School campus and started his own school with the students and faculty that had come with him from Lake Grove. The school was based in the therapeutic practice of Gestalt therapy and emphasized discipline and personal responsibility. It also concentrated on the ability to stay focused and present in the moment. One would be encouraged during sessions to "put both feet on the ground" or to "feel your butt sitting in the chair" as an exercise to stay grounded in the moment.

The school was also heavily based in structure and discipline. Each dorm of students was looked after by dorm parents, one of whom always lived in the adjoining staff apartment. We were never left totally alone and became very connected as a dorm. There were twenty to twenty-four kids in each dorm, and the rooms each had two beds, two nightstands, two chairs, and two wooden wardrobes. The walls were cinder block, and each room had a different color scheme, and there was a large room on the first floor that we called the Lobby. All of our group meetings as a dorm were held in the Lobby. We'd gather there to listen to music or just hang out.

When Leah enrolled me at the school, she had the forethought to actually *read* the entire contract before signing it. In the enrollment agreement, there was a clause that allowed for the school to make the decision to use psychotropic medication on a student if they saw fit. Leah crossed that section out before signing the document, telling them that she lived close enough to the campus to be able to get there fairly quickly if I were to have some sort of a crisis. Thank G-d she did that. Not that I ever needed that type of intervention, but I do wonder how many other kids there may not have been as lucky as I was to be spared that.

Although we'd thought I'd be coming home for occasional weekends and holidays, we soon found out that wasn't the case. Those weekends and vacations were only for the students who were much further along in the DeSisto program and had "earned" the time with good behavior. Certainly not for me as a new student there. I wouldn't go home until the following Thanksgiving, some fourteen months later. During vacation time when school wasn't officially in session, there would be various "camps" and trips offered to us—for an extra fee of course, and only if your therapist and other school officials felt like you were ready and capable. In the summers, there were bicycle trips with staff supervision, and trips to Mexico and Europe as well. There were also summer programs offered to students who were staying on campus, as I did. I participated in the musical theater program, because what else would I do? It was always the natural fit for me.

Then there were the electives that one could choose to do during the regular school year, like art, photography, and music. One semester I chose the songwriting elective, where we all wrote our own songs. I can't for the life of me remember what song I wrote. I do remember being asked to sing one of the songs that the teacher had written and recording the vocal in the studio for him. It was the first time I'd been behind a microphone in a real recording studio, and it wouldn't be the last. The proverbial show business bug had taken a large chunk of my heart, and still holds it today.

But there was a much darker side to this school. Many of the kids there were court-ordered and some of them had just come out of mental hospitals. The behaviors that I witnessed there were like nothing I'd ever seen before: kids were held down physically by staff members and many kids were overly medicated. We called it the Thorazine shuffle. Some kids ran away. Some attempted suicide. There were even a couple that succeeded.

I stayed at DeSisto for two and a half years, leaving in January of 1985 in what was supposed to be my senior year of high school. My senior year didn't resemble anything I'd read about in all my teenage romance novels. There were no school dances and no weekly football games. On Saturday nights, most of the students were either in their dorms or at an on-campus activity. I was assigned the duty that night of being in charge of the hourly official roll call of our dormmates. I had to physically see the individual to mark them as "present." We called it dorm check. That night there was a big snowstorm, which was a frequent occurrence and didn't stop on-campus activities like Movie Night at the Mansion from taking place. I made my way through the storm up to the Mansion to count my fellow dormmates for dorm check, and as I was leaving the Mansion it occurred to me. I realized that I had a golden opportunity. I was in possession of the clipboard containing the dorm check, and nobody would be looking for it until the next hourly check. If it were to be missed, it would likely not be for an hour or so. I could just split right that *second* and no one would be the wiser. I made a split-second decision, and, tucking the clipboard underneath a chair, I headed out into the snowy night.

Once I got down to the main road, I hitchhiked to a nearby bus stop and called Leah. She had long since been disenchanted by the school. She'd never quite forgiven the fact that she'd been sold a bill of goods in regard to some of the practices of the school. Among them was the fact that once she'd dropped me off in the fall of 1982, she thought I'd be coming home for vacations. Soon enough I had been there for a year or so without coming home once. By that time, I was comfortable at DeSisto and had drunk the proverbial Kool-Aid. She was ready for me to come home for good, but I'd wanted to stay. We agreed that if I changed my mind, she'd come and get me right away.

Now I told Leah that I was ready to come home. The trouble was that the snowstorm made it so she couldn't come and get me. I had to call the school and return for the night. My fellow dormmates were less than pleased, because my departure had led to them being "group leashed," which was exponentially worse than being leashed one-to-one. Group leashing meant you couldn't go anywhere without a group of four from your dorm, and my dorm mates kept me up all night yelling at me. I had to stay in the lobby all night long and wasn't allowed back into my room to pack up my belongings. When Leah arrived in the morning to pick me up, I got in the car, and we went home.

When I returned back to the hallowed halls of Northampton High School to reenroll, my transcripts from DeSisto were akin to swiss cheese. They had big, gaping holes everywhere.

Virtually none of the classes that I had taken at DeSisto were transferable, and I was many credits shy of graduating with my intended class. Later I would find out why the credits from DeSisto didn't transfer. The school wasn't fully accredited. I was put back into the junior class as a result.

And DeSisto School? It would run into major issues with the Commonwealth of Massachusetts over what the school was licensed for in the late 1990s. It would finally close in 2004. It turned out that the people who were running the place and dispensing psychotropic medicine had no idea what they were doing. Over the years, the kids who were attending differed from the ones that were there when I was. Kids in the nineties who were there were dramatically more ill-behaved and dramatically more medicated. There was one girl who'd been overmedicated and ended up in a hospital.

Transitioning back to life at Northampton High School as a junior—when all my friends were seniors and starting to talk about graduation and plans for the next year—was a bitter pill for me to swallow. It was simply too much for me to bear. My eighteenth birthday was approaching at the end of April, and the thought of facing another whole year of high school sounded less than appealing to me.

On the morning of my eighteenth birthday, April 26, 1985, I strolled into the main office and quit school. One signature on one page, and I was free. Then, I rented a single apartment and got a job making sandwiches at Subway. After that, I worked at Dunkin' Donuts, and at the town twenty-four-hour convenience store.

When I was working at Subway, I became friendly with a guy named Paul from a neighboring town. Paul was looking to move out on his own, and we agreed to share my new apartment. It was a one-bedroom, but the kitchen was big enough to curtain off a section for a bed, which became my spot. We lived there happily for a while, getting drunk and crazy and generally having way too much fun. Paul was also dabbling in some leisurely drug dealing which, in such a small town, soon became an issue. By the spring of 1986, Leah called me over to her house. She'd heard some rumors around town about the things Paul had been doing, and my name had been mentioned. She issued me a stern warning. Now she was telling me I should take a trip out to California and stay with Grandma Bess for a while.

This didn't feel like punishment. I couldn't have been more excited. I threw everything I could into my maroon American Tourister suitcase. I was just a few weeks short of my nineteenth birthday. When the plane was landing in LA, I looked out the window and saw the lights of my hometown twinkling below. I was home.

CHAPTER 14

I HEADED STRAIGHT OUT TO GRANDMA'S TOWN-house, a familiar place to me for sure. I'd missed her so much. She'd sent me care packages at DeSisto filled with See's Candies lollipops and special notes inside. I'd looked forward to those packages when I was at school, and now I was here with her in person. Things were definitely looking up.

On my nineteenth birthday, a few weeks later, I was in Grandma Bess's townhouse when her telephone rang. Picking up the receiver, I heard a man's voice on the other end of the line. I couldn't quite make out what he was saying. After a few seconds, his gibberish turned into understandable English, and the man identified himself as Denny. He'd been speaking mugwump to me, I figured out later. He'd somehow thought I'd understand it. Perhaps by osmosis? I don't know, but here was Denny on the phone. To this day, I don't know how he figured out I was there.

He'd been filming a documentary that day about the Mamas and the Papas with John and Michelle Phillips. It was the first time that they had all been together since my mom's funeral, and they were going to dinner together that night. Did I want to join them?

Did I want to join them? I did. I really only knew Michelle, and it sounded like a fun thing to do, so I accepted the invitation. I didn't know how to drive yet, so Grandma Bess dropped me off at the Imperial Gardens restaurant on Sunset Boulevard. Michelle had said she'd bring me home.

Everyone was sitting around a table in a private room upstairs. They all waved at me and said hello. I suddenly felt a little shy. "How old are you now?" someone asked me. It was the first time we'd all been together with me as an adult, the last time being on that sad, hot August day in 1974 when I was a grieving little girl.

"Oddly enough, today is my birthday," I said. "I'm nineteen." It occurs to me now that I was only a few years younger than my mother was when they all met in New York.

On the drive home that night, Michelle and I had a long talk. She told me that on the way to the restaurant that night, she and John and Denny had ridden together in one car. Knowing that I was coming to dinner, Michelle remarked to the two men in the backseat that she was surprised that nobody had ever figured out who my biological father was. Michelle said that Denny and John had looked at each other, and said, "Oh, you don't *know*?" Because apparently, they did. They knew his name and knew that he'd played with the band in the summer of 1966.

This was more information than I'd ever known about him. I'd always wondered about him, always dreamed that he would come and rescue me after my mother died. Who was he? Where was he? I wanted to find out more. Michelle agreed to help me find him.

Moving to California made it obvious that I needed to learn a few things, among them how to drive a car. I was nineteen in LA without a way to get myself around the city other than the limited public bus system. I needed to get my license. Grandma didn't think she was the right person to teach me, so she hired a driver's ed teacher from Sears Driving School, which did the trick. Grandma was still in the throes of handling my mother's estate, which was still open twelve years after her death. As the executor of the estate, she was able to withdraw the funds to buy me a sturdy used car, a maroon 1980 Datsun B-210. I named it Debbie the Datsun.

I hadn't stayed in touch with many of my Los Angeles friends. It was much harder to keep in touch with people in the 1980s than it is today, in the era of Facebook and social media. Misty was in college in Pennsylvania by that point, but once I was settled at Grandma's, I reached out to the two people that I still was in contact with. One was Chynna and the other one was Moon. In the years since we'd been at Oakwood together,

Moon had become well-known for her legendary Valley Girl lyric and performance on her dad's song "Valley Girl." Valley Girl had long been one of the many "voices" Moon had perfected while watching some of the more ridiculous girls who were around us in those days. And, yes, we hung out at the Sherman Oaks Galleria, the mall seen in the movies *Valley Girl* and *Fast Times at Ridgemont High*. All the time. Fer sure, fer sure.

Grandma loved to take the occasional trip to Las Vegas to play the nickel slot machines with her friend Ann. Ann and Grandma Bess were good friends, and even played mah-jongg together on weekends. They'd leave on Friday afternoons and return on Sunday nights, leaving me to my own devices. Taking advantage of the independence, I began looking through Grandma's record albums. Grandma had all of my mom's albums and a record player. My education began by listening to my mom's records. Among the first ones that I played was her final album, *Don't Call Me Mama Anymore*: the record I remembered being there for when it had been recorded in Chicago. The record started to play, the drumroll began, and the announcer said, "Ladies and gentlemen, Mister Kelly's is proud to present, Cass Elliot!" The band started to play, and my mother began to address the audience. Her voice, that voice I hadn't heard in so many years, was instantly recognizable to me as my mom's voice washing over me like a warm wave of water. Comforting, safe, and familiar. I must have spent weeks, collectively over many of Grandma's Vegas trips, listening to the records my mom made. It felt good to feel connected to my mom, after all the time that had passed.

I suppose I knew at that point that I wanted to try to do something in music. I just didn't know how to start. "We Are the World" had been a gigantic hit that year, the format consisting of various uber-successful musical artists coming together for one philanthropic cause, famine relief in Africa. I loved the record, and its mission was also important to me. I emotionally applauded the concept, as it appealed to the hippie child in me. And it also gave me an idea of my own.

I'd gone to school with so many of what we called the Second Generation, kids of the hippies of the sixties. We'd gone to one private school or another in LA, and a lot of us knew each other either through school or through our parents. I'd seen Chynna Phillips a few times at our respective birthdays over the years before I moved to Massachusetts. One day I went over to Michelle's house, where Chynna was living in the guest suite below the main house. We were sitting in her room when I told her of my idea.

"Hey, I've got this cool idea," I said. "We've got all these friends whose parents were sixties' musicians. Why don't we get together and write a song about drug abuse and record it for a charity?"

Chynna thought it could be interesting, and we started calling everyone we could think of. Moon Zappa was a hard no, and so were Donovan Leitch and Ione Skye, kids of the British singer Donavan. We must have called others, too, before the final call Chynna made to her friend Carnie Wilson and her sister, Wendy, whom I'd known from Oakwood. Carnie and Wendy were also interested in our idea, and before long we were sitting in Wendy's bedroom in front of her stereo singing harmony on Heart's "Dog and Butterfly." Carnie patiently taught us the parts over and over again until we got it right. We spent many afternoons singing and rehearsing together for the next couple of months, sometimes at Carnie and Wendy's mom's house in Encino, sitting cross-legged on their in-ground trampoline. Sometimes we'd rehearse at Chynna's place at her mom's house instead.

One afternoon Michelle overheard us singing and was duly impressed. She decided it was time to pull some Mama Michelle strings. She called up a friend of hers, record producer Richard Perry of the Pointer Sisters hits and many more, and arranged for the four of us to sing for Richard at his house high above Sunset Boulevard in the Hollywood Hills.

We arrived there all together one night, pressed the button at the driveway security gate, and headed up to the house where we were ushered inside to the den. Richard came in shortly after we got settled. We introduced ourselves and started to sing for him. We started with "Wild Heart" by Stevie Nicks, four notes, four words in perfect four-part harmony.

"Dare my wild heart . . ." He stopped us right there; that was all he needed to hear, I guess. Within a day he had set us up with a producer he worked with named Jim Tract, and the four of us were in the studio recording demos before we even really knew what had happened.

Michelle called me one afternoon and told me she had found Chuck Day, my biological father. She'd put classified ads in various magazines for musicians, one in a magazine appropriately called *Musician*. Her ad read, "Chuck Day, guitar player for the Mamas and the Papas. Please call Dotty" with a phone number included. She got a response fairly quickly from a friend of Chuck's. When they spoke on the phone, the first thing the friend asked was, "Is this about the kid?" Apparently, this stranger knew more about me than I knew about my own father.

Chuck was now living in Northern California, in Marin County. Michelle bought me a ticket to fly up there and meet him. I was terrified and excited all at once. Fortunately for me, my mom's first cousin Deah, whom I adored and felt safe with, lived in San Francisco. I knew I'd be okay as long as she was with me, and we arranged the first meeting with Chuck to take place at her apartment.

When the doorbell rang, and Chuck Day walked in, I knew instantly that we were connected though I still struggle to articulate exactly how that felt. When I looked at him, I saw my nose. It's hard to express just how weird that is. I'd constantly been asked, "Who did your nose?"—such an LA question—because for a girl who comes from such Jewishness to have a small schnozz is usually the result of a very talented plastic surgeon. But not me.

Chuck told me about the night I was conceived. There had only been one time that he and my mom had "been together." He told me about the concert they'd played at Forest Hills that day, and of all the Chinese food and drink he and my mom consumed that night. He also told me that my mom had not told him about my existence until I was around three years old. He'd asked to see me, and she agreed under the condition that he not tell me he was my father. She wasn't interested in having him be a part of my life, nor did she need him to be. She made that clear to him. He also told me that he'd been at my mom's funeral, standing across the street from all the activity. Afraid and overwhelmed, he didn't make any contact with me that day. I found it very hard to understand that—not that I would have had any idea how to deal with him on that day when I was seven, but it still irks me that he didn't walk over, if I'm being honest.

I want to spend a little bit of time telling Chuck's story, as it has its own interesting parts. Charles Wayne Day was born on August 5, 1942, in Chicago, Illinois, to a sixteen-year-old single mother. After our initial meeting, Chuck gave me her phone number. I reached out immediately. Although her given name was Frances, she went by the nickname of Frankye, and lived in the South with her girlfriend, Julie. We spoke frequently and got to know one another. But before feeling entirely comfortable speaking with me, she made me promise to "not to write a book and talk about her before she was dead." The idea of writing a book was not on my horizon or even in my fantasy, but she was insistent that her life be private. She still lived in a world where she had concerns about people finding out that she and Julie weren't only friends, they were life partners. They had been in an exclusive relationship for close to thirty years. She and Julie lived in Augusta, Georgia, and Julie worked for the city. How tragic that she had to worry about being outed as a gay woman.

On our many telephone calls, Frankye told me her story bit by bit. She told me that she'd known at a very early age that she was attracted to girls. She'd been confused by these feelings, and in an attempt to change how she felt, she'd become promiscuous. She told me that she'd slept with multiple boys, and soon discovered that she was pregnant. She was fifteen. Upon finding out about the pregnancy, Frankye told me that her mother had been acquainted with a couple who were childless, and they were happy to adopt the newborn. And, although he was adopted and raised by the Days, Chuck grew up knowing Frankye, and knowing he was her biological son. I can't imagine how confusing this must have felt for him.

Chuck began to demonstrate musical prowess at a young age, and he recorded and put out his first single at fifteen. "Pony Tail Partner" was released on Federal Records in 1957, and by 1965, he had relocated to Los Angeles. He played with

Johnny Rivers and maintained to the end of his life that he had been the one who had come up with the guitar riff intro to Rivers's hit song "Secret Agent Man." He said that he had based the idea for the riff on the theme to the popular television series *Peter Gunn*.

Chuck had been married while he'd still lived in Chicago. They had long since divorced, and Chuck had a daughter from that marriage. I had a half sister. A real half sister, named Rachelle, born in 1964. It felt like a dream come true, after all the years of feeling alone, that I had a half sister. Rachelle lived outside of Portland, Oregon. It wasn't long before Chuck gave me her phone number, and I called her right away. When she answered the phone with a speaking voice uncannily as low in timbre as my own, I knew we were related. When we met in person finally, the physical resemblance was there too. We shared the same nose and the same smile. We also shared the common feeling of not having any sort of relationship with the man whose DNA bound us together. I think we were just happy we found one another.

When I left San Francisco, I stayed in touch with Chuck from time to time, but it was always awkward. We had a very complicated relationship. By the time we met, I was nearly an adult and didn't know what kind of space he could occupy in my life. I had spent my life not knowing who my biological father was, but I did have a dad. Russ had stepped into that role. The way I learned to compartmentalize it was as such: Chuck was my actual biological *father*, which on a good day, anyone knows, takes only a few minutes to accomplish. But being a dad takes a lot longer, a lifetime. Russ was the one who I flipped my middle finger up to under the kitchen table, who saw me and sent me to my room when I'd been rude and backtalked. He did the real work.

Four-part harmony is a bitch. And Stephen Stills is right: being in a group might be the worst. I wouldn't know all of that until much, much later. But for now, here we were in the studio together, and the holidays were coming up. I had plans to go home to Massachusetts for the holidays and had told everyone in advance. I begged them not to record anything until I got back. When I returned, though, something didn't feel right when I spoke to the girls. What I didn't know was that in my absence it had been decided that I should not be in the group. The blend wasn't there—my voice was too loud.

Now I needed another plan. I called the only other person I knew in LA, Moon. She suggested that I check out an acting class that she'd taken previously and enjoyed. The class was located at the Beverly Hills Playhouse on Robertson Boulevard and was taught by a coach named Lynette Katselas. I enrolled in the class and started going twice a week. I met some new friends and began socializing and enjoying this new chapter, even though a big part of me was still upset about the girls and the group. I was crushed and disappointed to have been edged out of something that I had helped create, but I was a Cohen, after all, and Cohens always survive.

———■———

I'd loved being with Grandma Bess, but I needed more freedom and the ability to have friends over whenever I wanted. I also wanted to live closer to my friends, who were mostly living on the city side of the hills. I'd developed a habit of staying out very late hanging out with friends, and the drive back to Sun Valley was long and arduous at night. I'd get home at one or two in the morning and pull into my parking space directly across from Grandma's townhouse. Getting out of my car, I would hear the sounds of Grandma's radio coming through her open, upstairs windows. "She's gone to sleep, listening to the baseball game again," I'd think to myself.

However, by that time of the evening, or morning, the AM radio station that carried the baseball games had switched over to a Top 40 format. I'd come home to songs like Madonna's "Like a Virgin" playing loudly through the complex. Letting myself into the townhouse, I'd go upstairs and switch the radio off, each time fearing that I'd wake her up in the process, but I never did. Grandma was a sound sleeper.

I did want to move out, so Grandma helped me find a studio apartment on Cahuenga Boulevard. She even cosigned the lease and helped me get settled in. I had a stereo with a turntable set up on makeshift shelves I'd built from cinder blocks and long wooden planks, and I'd sit in that room and listen to music for hours on end. Mostly, I was listening to Whitney Houston and other pop music of the time, but on this day, it was my mom's *Bubblegum, Lemonade* album I was concentrating on—in particular, the song "Lady Love," which I was listening to for the first time. When I heard the beginning of the song and my mom's sweet dedication to me, my emotions almost overwhelmed me. I missed her more right then, hearing her voice talking about me, than I had ever remembered missing her before, and oddly, I felt even closer to her as a result.

I was still taking the acting class in Beverly Hills, where I developed a minor crush on one of the other students. He'd recently had surgery for a pesky hernia and was recovering at home. I went over to visit him one night at a guest house in Beverly Hills. A couple of other kids from our acting class were there, trying in vain to cheer him up. There was this geeky weird guy who annoyed me, and also a kid named Jack, who was an okay guy. I felt kind of neutral toward him. All of a sudden, our surgical friend threw us all out, saying he was in pain. As we left the kid's place, I felt badly that we'd all gotten kicked out unceremoniously and suggested to the weird guy and Jack that we go for coffee together. When they both accepted the offer, I realized I'd made a huge faux pas. I really didn't like the weird guy, and I was instantly sorry I'd invited him. Now, I had a problem. So, I grabbed Jack's arm and said to him under my breath, "Let's lose this turkey. Follow me."

Jumping into our respective cars, we headed out into the streets with me running red lights and trying to lose weird guy, whom I think we ditched somewhere up on Mulholland Drive. Jack and I ended up back at my apartment drinking coffee until the sun came up. And listening to music, talking, becoming friends. Jack was funny and sweet. I liked him a lot—that much I already knew. By the time my twentieth birthday came around a couple of weeks later, we'd become much more than just friends.

CHAPTER 15

WHEN JUNE OF 1986 ROLLED AROUND, I WAS thrilled to learn that Misty was moving back to LA. She'd decided to transfer from Villanova to UCLA in the fall. More importantly, she and I had decided to move in together and get an apartment on the city side of LA, near where she'd be working. I'd been living at the same studio apartment that Grandma had cosigned the lease for a couple of years before. I was horrible at keeping my place clean, even ignoring the mess in the kitchen to the point where I shut the kitchen door and never went back inside it. I didn't get my security cleaning deposit back—let's just put it that way. I must have inherited that tendency my mother had for being messy.

Misty and I found a place on Orange Street, near Crescent Heights Boulevard, that we both loved. We moved in over the summer and got settled. The apartment buildings on our new street were built close together, with driveways in between. We got to know our new neighbors in the building, and in the one next door. We had quite a party over there on Orange Street.

Another bonus for me was that our new apartment was near where Jack was living, and we were still dating. We spent a lot of time together when he wasn't working at his waiter job in Westwood. Jack had dreams and aspirations of being a record producer and songwriter one day, like his father had been before him.

Jack's father was a man named Marty Kugell, and he'd been the producer of a song by the Five Satins called "In the Still of the Night," one of the biggest songs of the fifties. It was written and recorded in the basement of a church in New Haven, Connecticut, where they lived. The song had been originally released on Marty's record label, which he called Standord Records. It became such a big hit that it was hard to keep up with the demand for it. Jack told me that Marty had known he needed help getting the record out more efficiently. He took the record into New York City and secured a deal with a larger record company, Ember Records. Not fully understanding the difference between wholesale and retail, he signed a contract that gave him only the tiniest of percentages. Marty still had quite a few of the records back in New Haven, and they would need new labels put on them before they were sold. Marty brought the new labels home, and the labels were then affixed to cover the Standord label. There are a few of these 45s still around today. If you know anyone with an "In the Still of the

Night" record, see if there's a Standord label under the Ember one. It's a major collectible item.

Marty decided to move his young family to Los Angeles in the summer of 1981 to pursue his career on the West Coast. Before the family was truly settled, he had a major heart attack in November of the same year and was hospitalized. He would not recover and passed away very soon afterward. Losing a parent was one of the things that Jack and I had in common.

Meanwhile, I worked a series of completely meaningless jobs, like busing tables at a café in Beverly Hills and working the cash register at a twenty-four-hour diner. I turned twenty-one that next April. Renting a limo for the night, Jack and I cruised around LA blasting the Beastie Boys. Damn right we had a right to party, and that we did.

Even though I wasn't living with Grandma Bess anymore, I was in touch with and saw her constantly. I called her to check on her frequently. On more than one occasion her phone would give me the busy signal, indicating that the line was in use.

I'd dial her phone number again. Still busy. Dial it again, busy. Dial. Busy. Trying not to let my imagination run wild and think terrible thoughts. I'd try it again, STILL BUSY. Panic would then set in, and I would jump in my car and speed over the hill as fast as I could. Taking the canyon roads and getting out to the townhouse fifteen miles away in record time, I'd arrive at Grandma's.

Sun Valley in the late eighties was much less safe than it was when Grandma first moved to her beloved townhouse. She'd made some changes to her unit, knocking out the wall separating the small living room from the dining room to create one large room. She'd also installed iron bars on all of the downstairs windows, and a screened door with a heavy-duty deadbolt on the front door, as a security measure. When I would pull up in my car, I could hear the television on the street through the screen door, usually broadcasting a Dodgers game. Using my key to open the heavy door, I'd then walk into the living area to discover Grandma, sitting in her reclining chair watching TV.

Grandma had a cordless phone that she would simply *forget* to turn off when she'd finished her call. She'd just put the phone down on the table when she was done, and that was that. She'd almost never realized that she'd done it, until I showed up with a look on my face that she eventually learned to recognize. Looking around without saying a word to her, I'd locate the remote phone and click it to the off position.

"Did I do it *again?*" she'd ask me. "Yes, Grandma," I'd say, reassuringly telling her how much I loved her, and that it was okay. It was just one of those things she had a hard time figuring out, new technology and all. She eventually did, after many crazed drives of mine over that hill.

My mother's estate would remain insolvent and in an open state until 1987. By then a new format for listening to music—the compact disc—had been invented. The sound of a CD was far superior to what cassette tapes or records had offered before. The original recorded tapes had to be accessed, mixed, and processed using the new technology. People were so eager to hear their favorite music in new, clean, hiss-free formats that they repurchased entire catalogs of music on CD, even if they already owned the records in another format.

And therein lay the miracle that saved my mother's estate. The wording in most record contracts from that time covered known formats at the time of contractual obligation, with no provisions made for future inventions. It's different today: now contracts contain a "future format clause" to cover delivery methods that haven't been invented yet. But back in the late 1980s, every artist who wanted to participate in the CD revolution had to sign addendums to their original contracts allowing the label to release their music on CD. As I was over the age of eighteen at that point, I was the one who signed the addendum. That meant that new royalty checks began to come in. And for us, that meant that outstanding bills could finally be paid. In 1987, thirteen years after my mother died, her estate could officially be closed.

After the estate was finally settled, there was a little money that I could use to put a down payment on a condo that was located in the same complex that Grandma Bess lived in. This way, I'd be close to her and have my independence at the same time.

With the idea of wanting to be a singer still lodged in my lofty little brain, I tried every avenue suggested to me. I played my simple demo tape to whoever would listen. One of my mother's close friends from back in the Greenwich Village days, a comedian named Lotus Weinstock, suggested that she could send the tape to a friend of hers for his opinion, a man named Roy Silver. Yes, the very same Roy Silver who had managed my mother in the Big 3 and the Mugwumps so many years ago.

Roy got in touch with me immediately and agreed to be my manager. A handshake deal. No physical agreement, and either one of us could terminate the relationship at any time. He was sure he'd be able to get me a record contract, and he set about "getting it done." He'd even begun sending the *Los Angeles Times* music critic, Robert Hilburn, a weekly update letter on how he was planning to make it all happen.

Roy was in his late fifties by now, married, and living nearby. He developed his plan for me according to what he believed I should and should not do, and he was rather strident about it. After a short while I didn't want to play with Roy anymore, and I told him so. He was less than happy with me, but the last thing I wanted or needed was someone bossing my bossy self around.

I had stayed in touch with Carnie after we stopped singing together, and we forged an incredibly close friendship over the years. She, Wendy, and Chynna had decided to call their group Wilson Phillips, using their collective last names. They had been writing and recording songs and had signed a lucrative record contract with a small but powerful record company in New York called SBK Records. Carnie would play me the demo tapes they were making, and it was instantly clear how unique and beautiful their blend was.

Wilson Phillips was a huge success. The record company spared no expense in promoting the three girls, and it paid off, with the first album selling over 10 million copies worldwide in 1990. My childhood friends were bona fide pop stars. I was and am one of their biggest fans.

Was I envious? Of course. You bet your ass I was. But envy made me more determined to succeed.

Unceremoniously, I rode the coattails of Wilson Phillips into my own recording contract under the tutelage of music business veteran Artie Mogull. Artie had at one time been partners with the very same guys in New York that had become SBK, home to Wilson Phillips. Artie was branching out on his own and now had a production company. Roy Silver and Artie had long been friends, and Roy had recently given Artie my demo tape, even though he was no longer my manager. As it turned out, Artie was eager to sign me.

Though I was over the moon about the deal, I was not happy that Roy was back on the scene, and as the negotiations were finalized, Roy was paid a lump sum of money and sent on his way. Though the ending of that relationship was not ideal, I did meet Roy many years later for lunch and set things right.

He'd long since forgotten all the details of our disagreement and was happy to see me. I was grateful to have been able to say I'm sorry and thank you to him before he passed away a couple of years later.

In 1991, I signed my production deal with Artie and the production company he was working with, Ventura Music Group. Ventura Music Group had a production deal with MCA Records, the very same company that had the Mamas and the Papas and my mom's solo catalog. My record would come out on the same label my mom's records were on. Traversing the hallways of MCA past huge pictures of all their artists, including ones of the group with my mom's smiling face, was one of the most amazing things I've experienced.

This was the big time.

I started meeting with songwriters and record producers in search of the right songs and direction to take. One was Diane Warren, known for songs that she'd written for many artists, including "I Get Weak" by Belinda Carlisle of the Go-Go's and "Nothing's Gonna Stop Us Now" by Jefferson Starship. We met in the RCA Building on Sunset Boulevard in Hollywood. My mom had recorded her first record for RCA in the legendary studios in that building, and now here I was walking almost in her literal footsteps, on ground she'd traversed herself.

I met Diane at her office on the eighth floor, and she mentioned that she'd "heard" of me quite recently. She had been up in Marin County, working with a well-known songwriter and record producer named Walter Afanasieff. Leaving Walter's studio to go back to her hotel one night, she was picked up by a taxi driver who seemed to know about Walter and his work. He began to tell her all about himself, that he was a guitar player and a singer-songwriter himself. He'd had somewhat of a career for himself back in the sixties. He'd also fathered a child with Mama Cass. It was Chuck Day, of course.

Life is strange.

I instantly connected with Diane. Anyone who knows her knows she is the most compassionate, animal-loving, funniest, and potty-mouthed individual on Earth. She had an even filthier mouth that I did, which is saying a lot. I loved her immediately. She had a couple of songs that she thought would be right for me. And she agreed to produce the songs for my record, along with her production partner, a man named Guy Roche. They had a studio around the corner from Diane's office, and it was there that we started to work together on my project. The amount of fun we had is evidenced in pictures that I have promised Diane I would never show anyone.

I was also set up with songwriters in an effort to encourage me to co-write a song or two for the record. One of the people I had been working with had a writing room located at Sunset Sound studios in Hollywood. One afternoon, the receptionist greeted me and told me that Graham Nash of Crosby, Stills & Nash was also at the studio that day. He'd apparently heard that I'd been working in another room there and had left word for me to come and say hello. I went into the studio to find him. He led me from the control room to the floor of the studio, where the wooden floors had rows and rows of large tape reels running the width of the floor. Graham explained that he was in the midst of choosing the songs for an extensive CD box set that was set to be released. "This is all because of your mother," he said, before raising his middle finger toward the ceiling and saying lovingly, "Fuck you, Cass!"

After I got the record contract, it was time to find a manager. After meeting with a few different companies, I signed with Peter Asher Management. Peter had been an artist himself, as a member of the British sixties act Peter and Gordon, and had long managed the successful careers of artists such as James Taylor and Linda Ronstadt. I'd known Peter since I was younger because Russ had played with both of those artists for years. It felt like home to me. A great manager from his office, Ira Koslow, was assigned to watch over me. I felt like I would be properly looked after. Mostly I felt comfortable because they were all friends with Russ, who I had been able to rekindle a relationship with after moving back to Los Angeles. He had remarried recently and he and his wife, Nicolette Larson, had welcomed a baby girl in the summer of 1990. They named her Elsie May, and nothing was more fun to me than playing with that sweet baby.

CHAPTER 16

I N THE SUMMER OF 1991, JACK AND I HAD BEEN DATING
for four years and living together for two. We'd rented a
house in Studio City, which was still nearby to Grandma's
house, should she need me. It felt like I needed to be within
a fifteen-minute drive. If she left that portable phone off the
hook again, I'd be there quickly to correct it.

Jack had been working for a music industry trade magazine
called *Hitmakers*, which was like *Billboard* magazine for the
radio programmers who assembled radio station playlists. He
was constantly bringing home promotional copies of the new-
est, high-priority current music.

I was getting antsy. I wanted to get married, but Jack was
hesitant. He hadn't established himself in his career yet, and
he wanted more stability in his life before making the commitment. My feeling was that if he didn't know if he wanted
to marry me after four years together, I might not stick around
much longer.

The day after July 4, 1991, I was at our house in Studio City with my friend Jill Schwartz, who had also been in the acting class where Jack and I had met. Jill and I were in the living room when Jack came home with two boxes of Cracker Jacks, one in his hand, open, and one still sealed in the other. He was eating out of his box and tossed me the other one, telling me to open it. Not wanting to open the second one unnecessarily, I asked him for some of his, out of the already open box. He told me to open mine instead. "No, give me some of yours," I said. "NO. Open *yours*." This continued for a while until, grumbling, I finally opened my Cracker Jack box and began to eat.

"What's your prize?" Jack asked. Digging through the box, I located it, and opened it. It was a ring. Taking it out of the paper, I realized it had much more weight to it than a silly plastic ring. This was real, and Jill started yelling at Jack, "Get down on your knee, you jerk!" He did, and he asked me to marry him. I accepted on the spot. We started to plan a wedding and put down a hefty deposit at the Hotel Bel-Air. At the same time, I began to record my record.

Partway through the record, I started to have doubts about everything. I wondered if I had made a gigantic mistake. I woke up one day, took my ring off, left it on the nightstand, and checked into the Chateau Marmont in Hollywood, near the studio I was working at on Fairfax. We were recording at Cherokee Studios, which had been around for years.

When I got back to the Chateau that night after recording, there were a hundred long-stemmed red roses in my hotel suite. Jack came over to the hotel and we talked for hours. I was the asshole. I was the chicken. I had gotten cold feet, and I knew I'd made a mistake. The runner. I stayed the night at the hotel, because I'd paid through the nose for the suite and I was going to enjoy it.

I got up early and put my ring back on, but I wasn't satisfied. I didn't want to wait anymore. I definitely didn't want that big wedding we had thought we wanted. I just wanted it done and over with, so an ultimatum was made. Marry me, now, or forget it. I suggested we go to Las Vegas. Jack agreed, as long as his family was cool with it.

He spoke with them, and they were okay with it as long as we were married by a rabbi. I didn't bother to call my family. I didn't feel as though I needed to; my mom was dead, and my biological father was a joke. Leah was all the way across the country in Massachusetts, and I didn't know where Russ was. I knew Grandma would be happy as long as I was happy.

I called Misty and told her I needed her to come to Las Vegas with me to be my witness. We'd promised each other so many years ago on the swing set in her backyard that we would be at one another's weddings as maid of honor. I ran to find a dress to wear, and two gold wedding bands, one for him and one for me. Jack called his brother, Fritz, and the four of us jumped on a plane. We landed in Las Vegas, went downtown, and got our marriage license. We checked into the Desert Inn

Hotel, where we had reserved a suite, and called the only rabbi we could find. We were married on November 5, 1991, just a few minutes before midnight.

On November 27, 1990, Japanese electronics giant Matsushita paid somewhere around $6 billion to acquire the MCA Corporation in one of the largest deals of its kind. By the following November, Matsushita had begun to "clear out" MCA's artist roster. They dropped a slew of artists in one fell swoop, with Belinda Carlisle, the teen sensation Tiffany, and yours truly among them.

When I had signed the deal, there had not been a formal budget set for the project, with the higher-ups saying that they would spend "whatever" was needed. They must have had high hopes that they could get in on the same action enjoyed by SBK Records with Wilson Phillips. But now my contract with MCA was over, more than halfway through the recording of the album. The tapes were shelved, and I was devastated.

CHAPTER 17

GRANDMA CALLED AND ASKED ME TO COME OUT TO
the townhouse and talk with her. She had something on
her mind and wanted to speak with me. When I got there,
she told me that she wanted to talk about having my mother's
remains moved from their current location in Baltimore to a
cemetery in Los Angeles. She told me that when my mother
had passed, it had been so sudden, and everyone had been so
traumatized. The days following my mom's death had been a
blur, and she'd felt pressured to bury my mother at one of the
big Los Angeles cemeteries. There had been so much press
attention and she'd even felt as if the prices were unfairly
inflated on some levels due to my mother's celebrity. "No,"
Grandma had decided. She would bring my mother home to
Baltimore and place her in the family plot next to her father.
My grandfather had been buried with his parents and siblings
in an Orthodox cemetery there, and my mom had been there
next to him since 1974.

Grandma told me that she regretted that I hadn't had the opportunity to visit my mom's final resting place, and now she wanted to rectify the situation and bring my mom's remains back to LA. We went to speak to a representative at Mount Sinai Memorial Park in the Hollywood Hills. The woman we spoke with there was lovely and took us to look at a couple of spaces that were available.

When we went back to her office to do the transfer paperwork, Grandma began to tell us how, when she passed away, she didn't want a fuss. She didn't want a big to-do. I felt my embarrassment rising. I asked the representative to excuse us for a few minutes, and she stepped out of the room. Turning my attention to Grandma, I admonished her gently. I assured her that when her time came, it wouldn't matter much what sort of celebration we'd have, but we'd need to do something, I reminded her how much I loved her, and that was the end of that conversation.

When my mom's remains were relocated, so was the original headstone. It shows my mother's legal name, Ellen Naomi Cohen. In the middle, below her legal name, it reads "Cass Elliot," with music notes around it.

For a few years that followed, her grave remained private, just for us. Before long, the location had been discovered and shared on the internet. I began to get accustomed to going to visit my mom's spot (I hate the word "grave," so I don't like to use it) and finding items left there in honor of my mom. Sometimes I would find flowers, at other times special stones and trinkets. I also find notes, some of them very personal. I used to feel strange when I'd find these items on my mother's headstone, in this once-private place where I had come to remember my mom. In time, I've come to understand something important. On that day at LAX when that fan stepped between us and asked for my mom's autograph, I had understood that I shared my mom. She didn't just belong to me. That was part of who she was, and it will always be that way. Even at the cemetery.

In 1993, Wilson Phillips had decided to take a break from each other. Chynna was recording a solo album, and Carnie and Wendy were keen to record as a duo. They had left the management team that had been working with Wilson Phillips, and they had hired a new manager named Mickey Shapiro. The same Mickey Shapiro who had been my mother's lawyer, back in the early seventies.

Carnie and I had remained close over the years. We had become thicker than thieves, spending days laughing like wild hyenas. Speeding around Los Angeles in Carnie's brand-new black BMW 850il, we would roll the windows down and scream the vilest of obscenities we could muster. From time to time, I worried that someone would recognize Carnie and our fun would be over. Wilson Phillips had been all over MTV and in magazines all over the world. But no one was the wiser, or at least so I thought.

Years later, at a function at my kids' school, a man, a proper Englishman, was telling people about a time that he'd been walking on a street when a dark car came up alongside him with the windows rolled down, and that the girl who sang in Wilson Phillips yelled filthy things at him. I laughed out loud and almost choked on my drink. I didn't elaborate on what I was laughing about, but I called Carnie that night and we howled. Busted!

Jack had stopped working at *Hitmakers*, and he had been working in Diane Warren's office as one of their assistants. He worked there during the days and was writing songs at home in the studio that we'd set up in an extra bedroom. We'd since moved into another rental house, and now had an extra room to dedicate to a music space.

It turned out that SBK wanted Carnie and Wendy to record a Christmas album, now that Chynna had taken the solo route. They set about choosing the songs and decided to write one original with Jack, as we'd all become such good friends and were supportive of one another. It was the middle of July, and they worked at our house, stringing Christmas lights in the studio and lowering the air conditioning to sixty-five degrees to get the mood right. They wrote the song that would be the title song of the Christmas album *Hey Santa!* Liking what he'd heard, Mickey Shapiro convinced SBK to allow Jack, a new producer and writer, the chance to produce a few songs on the album. Along with the opportunity to produce, Mickey also got Jack a music publishing deal. Although I'd given the music business the middle finger after my record deal fell apart, Jack was game to play with those people. At least someone would be working, because frankly, I'd had enough.

After finishing the record, we decided that a vacation was in order. At our wedding reception, Carnie had been seated next to Jack's best friend from high school, a guy named Steven Port. They had hit it off that night and had been dating for a couple of years now. We rented a beautiful house on Maui together, overlooking the blue Pacific Ocean. We swam in the pool on the property and spent our days in search of the legendary Maui Wowie. We never did find any, despite our best efforts.

We had been in Maui a few days when I heard from Grandma Bess that she wasn't feeling well. She'd been diagnosed with shingles. When we returned a few days later, I went to see her. She was in a great deal of pain. The doctor had prescribed Tylenol with codeine. With Grandma so sick, I felt helpless. I didn't know if I could take care of everything, so with Grandma's approval, I hired a woman through the Jewish Family Services to come every day to help.

After a few weeks, the rash from the shingles had disappeared, but the pain persisted. The doctors tried everything to relieve her from the pain she was in, including performing a nerve block on her spine. It was unsuccessful, and she was also developing bedsores from lack of movement. She needed more care than we could give her. The best option was for Grandma to go into a nursing home, so she went into a facility very close to where I was living. This way, I could be there every day with her, which I was.

I went to see her one day in December of 1993, and walked into her room. When I got close to give her a kiss, she grabbed my shirt. Drawing me closer to her, she said, "Get me out of here." I explained to her that it wasn't possible for her to go home to her townhouse by herself, and that she'd need to go to Leah's house in Massachusetts so that Leah would be able to take care of her. I can only imagine how hard it must have been for Leah, being all the way across the country when her mom had been so ill. Leah had been depending on me to help take care of Grandma, and I was now out of ideas. Leah and I had discussed it, and I made plans to bring Grandma to Massachusetts as soon as I could. I told Grandma of the plan, and she was happy to know she'd be out of the nursing home soon.

I went out to the townhouse to pack her suitcase. There weren't many items of clothing in her wardrobe that were suitable for East Coast winters, but I grabbed what I could find. Locking the doors tightly, I made sure that all the lights were off and the blinds closed.

When I got outside to my car and put Grandma's suitcase in the trunk, I noticed that the Southern California Gas Company truck was parked at the townhouse next door. "This must be meant to be," I thought to myself, approaching the technician. I asked him if he wouldn't mind coming over to

Grandma's before he left and turning off the gas line for me. "The unit will be vacant for a few months," I told him. "If there's an earthquake or anything, I won't have to rush right over." He extinguished the pilot lights on all of the gas appliances, and I thanked him and went home.

I booked Grandma and me first-class tickets to Massachusetts, necessary because Grandma's heels were inflamed and sore, and the footrests would allow her feet to be elevated. We arrived in Massachusetts and were safely at home in Northampton with Leah before long.

Leah got Grandma settled in, and I stayed through the holidays. One evening, I had gone out to see a friend, and had the local Top 40 on in the rental car. It was Christmas time, and the snow was falling. Suddenly I heard the familiar opening notes of "Hey Santa!" I could hardly believe it. Here I was, thousands of miles away, in a little Massachusetts town, hearing the song my husband and my good friends had written in our house, on the local radio station. I was so happy for everyone and couldn't wait to get home to celebrate the success with them.

Being home was great, but I hadn't anticipated how I'd feel about being so far away from Grandma. I stayed at home in California until my heart couldn't take it anymore. Flying back and forth between Massachusetts and California became an event that repeated itself every few weeks.

I was woken up in the early morning of January 17, 1994, at 4:30 a.m. to be exact, by the 6.7-magnitude Northridge earthquake. The sound of the earthquake, like a freight train barreling through the house, was almost as frightening as the shaking itself. It was terrifying, even for a native Californian. I'd felt earthquakes before, lots of them. This one had been much more severe, and the damage was widespread. Our rented house was a mess—the cabinets and refrigerator had opened, sending the contents crashing to the floor. Even the fishbowl on the counter had flown off and landed upside down on the carpet.

I was so glad I'd had the gas company turn off the gas at Grandma's townhouse. I went there a few days later and straightened the pictures that had shifted. There were a few cracks, but the place had held up well. I was so glad that she'd been in Massachusetts.

Grandma's pain from the shingles infection never went away, and she needed more care than we could provide at her house, so Leah made the painful decision to take Grandma to the Jewish nursing home. She was there for a couple of months before she had a stroke and was brought to the local hospital to recover. It wasn't looking good. Leah called me. I was at home in California and got on the first flight that I could.

I went to see her the day that I got to Northampton. She wasn't able to speak anymore, but her eyes were open. Her gaze was fixed, looking up at the ceiling and slightly to the left. I wondered if she was seeing something magical. Did she see her mom? Did she see Bubby waiting for her? I took her hand and told her how much I loved her. She'd been more than simply a grandmother to me; she'd been a Grand Mother. She'd protected me and loved me from day one, and I'd miss her every day. She died a day later, and we held a small service for her in Leah's living room. It was far from the big to-do Grandma had warned me about that day at Mount Sinai. I know she would have been happy about that.

Grandma's death hit me harder than my own mother's had. Maybe it was because I was older now and understood more. Maybe it was because I'd had so much more time with Grandma and was so close to her.

I hardly remember crying when my mom died. I know I didn't cry at her funeral, because I always felt like I'd been wrong *not* to. I didn't understand then what I do now about trauma, and how going through that type of tragedy can cause all sorts of different reactions in people, especially a young child. I think I shut off those feelings, perhaps in a subconscious effort to preserve my own sanity.

Losing Grandma was different. I found myself wanting to pick up the phone to tell her something about my day and realizing that she wasn't there to answer the call. While packing up her townhouse so that it could be sold, just being there and knowing she wasn't going to be coming back to the place she'd loved so much cut me to the core. I consoled myself by reminding myself that she was finally reunited with the love of her life—my grandfather, Philip—and with her daughter.

Grandma had confessed years before to me that losing her child—my mother—had been more difficult than losing her husband. She told me that it was unnatural, that a parent should never have to bury their child. It had broken her heart in a way that had never healed.

I had a dream a year or so after Grandma died. In the dream I was walking down a long hospital hallway and passed by a room with the door open. As I looked in the doorway, I saw Grandma sitting up in the hospital bed, smiling. I stopped and entered the room. I looked at her and said, "Hi." She looked back at me and smiled, not saying a word. I wanted to see if this was really happening, I told myself in the dream. Was she visiting me? There was only one way to find out.

"Are you happy?" I asked her, and she nodded. I needed more confirmation, so I continued. "Are you so happy, being with your husband and firstborn?" She smiled and nodded. I woke from that dream feeling settled. Grandma was at peace. Wherever they all were, they were together. That thought comforted me like my blankie had when I was little.

CHAPTER 18

IN THE SPRING OF 1997, *PEOPLE* MAGAZINE DECIDED to write an article about the kids of the Mamas and the Papas, and they wanted to take a picture of all of us together. We were all spread around the country, and the Doherty kids were in Canada. We were all flown to New York for a group photo shoot with photographer Neal Preston. Most of us knew one another, but it was the very first time we were all together. That fact, in and of itself, was fairly significant. Denny had accompanied his kids from Toronto, as they were still young enough to be living at home. Denny was armed with his home video camera, capturing everything. He must have had some sense of pride in seeing all of us Mamas and Papas "kids" hanging out together. We all stood together, leaning on one another, some of us holding hands. We all seemed like a sort of family bonded by "the strangeness of it all," as I told the *People* writer. It's still true today. We are all indeed bound in an unexplainable way.

The Rock & Roll Hall of Fame announced the inductees for the class of 1998 in October of 1997. The Mamas and the Papas were to be inducted the following January, along with fellow esteemed musical acts the Eagles and Fleetwood Mac. It was truly a celebration of the California sound. Years later, I'd learned that on the first night that Stevie Nicks had met Lindsay Buckingham at a party, he'd been strumming "California Dreamin'" on his guitar. She'd approached him, and bravely joined in song with him. The rest as they say, is . . . well, you know.

The Mamas and the Papas had officially been eligible for the nomination since the year 1990, denoting twenty-five years since their first commercial release in 1965. Every year, the Rock & Roll Hall of Fame's board has the task of deciding which of the many nominations received will make up that year's class of new inductees. The people who made up the board at the Rock & Roll Hall of Fame were well-respected and important executives in the music and entertainment industry. Among them was at least one executive with rumored unpleasant entanglements with John Phillips, enough to have made induction into the Hall of Fame an impossibility, until Michelle ran into one of these execs at a party one evening, taking the opportunity to sit on this man's lap and use her feminine wiles to her advantage. She asked him why the Mamas and the Papas weren't in the Rock & Roll Hall of Fame yet. He replied, "John did this

. . . and John did that," before she interrupted him and said, "OK, but what did Cass, Denny, or I ever do to you?" As he was unable to come up with an excuse, it's my understanding the nomination came shortly after the lap sitting.

In December of 1997, Russ's wife, Nicolette, died suddenly. Their little girl, Elsie, was only seven then. She was the very same age that I'd been when I lost my mom. The irony was far from lost on me, and I instantly empathized with Elsie. After Nicolette passed away, all of her family and all of us went back up to the house. People gathered in the kitchen and in the other main rooms. Elsie went off to her room to play with her cousins and watch cartoons. At some point that evening, I went to find her. She was in her room sitting on her bed, watching her TV, and I sat beside her. I remembered how I'd felt when I'd lost my mom, and I wanted to find some way of telling Elsie that I understood how she was feeling. Sitting a little bit closer to her, I told her that when I was exactly the same age as she was, my mommy had gone to live with G-d, just like hers had. I really understood, and that I was always going to be around if she ever wanted to talk. I loved her so very much. We could, and would, heal together in many ways.

The Rock & Roll Hall of Fame ceremonies were coming up in just a month. Arrangements were being made, and soon I was presented with a problem. The tickets were incredibly scarce. I was given a seat for myself and one for a guest. The problem was that I had two family members I felt should be in attendance besides myself: Leah and Joe, my aunt and uncle, my mother's sister and brother. To say nothing of the fact that there wouldn't be a seat for Jack. The producer of the Mamas and the Papas, Lou Adler, did an incredibly nice thing and gave me one of his extra tickets. This way, all three of us could attend. Although I was sad Jack couldn't be there with us, I flew to New York on January 11, 1998, the day before the ceremonies were to take place.

We were all staying at the Waldorf Astoria, where the ceremonies were also being held. Denny, his wife, Jeanette, and his kids were staying in the same hotel, as were John Phillips and his wife, Farnaz. Michelle was there, too. Leah drove down from Northampton, where she was still living, and stayed with me. Leah also wrote the speech for me to give at the ceremonies. I was grateful, because I didn't know what to say, and I definitely didn't want to screw this up. I wanted everything to be perfect. I'd bought a long dark red velvet dress and black velvet heeled boots for the event, and I'd chosen a necklace that'd belonged to my mom to wear with it. This way, part of my mom would be with me.

Everyone was sitting together at the ceremony that night, at tables next to one another dressed to the nines. Each act being honored had their own tables. I was regretting with all my heart my choice of footwear, the heeled boots becoming increasingly painful as the night wore on, when the tap on my shoulder came. It was almost our turn; time to go. I made a quick decision: the dress was floor-length, and no one would see my feet if I slouched a little. Taking my off my velvet boots and rolling them into a ball, I pretended they were an evening bag as we were escorted through the kitchen and behind the ballroom stage to the waiting area. When we arrived at the staging area on the side of the stairs, I gingerly put the boots back on. I could feel my nerves beginning to rise as I listened to Shania Twain talking about how the music of the Mamas and the Papas had affected her growing up. Then, she introduced the group and inducted them formally into the Rock & Roll Hall of Fame. As the crowd began to applaud, Michelle went up on the stage first, followed by John, and then Denny. I hesitated for a second, nervous. Denny grabbed my hand and led me up the steps.

Once we were on the stage, Denny stepped forward to the microphone amid the applause. He spoke of the honor of the occasion, and thanked his wife and his children, who were in the audience watching. Then, he paused, and said, "And, absent friends. Cass Elliot." The audience applauded in appreciation. "Whose daughter, Owen," he continued, gesturing to me, "has come up to receive the award for her mom." The clapping continued as John, whom I was standing next to, pulled me close and planted a kiss on my head as I grinned sheepishly. Denny leaned over and gave me a peck on the cheek before returning to the microphone, telling them that I hadn't wanted to come up, but that they'd dragged me up. He went on to thank his fellow Canadian, Shania Twain, for her introduction, and for that matter, *all* the Canadians. "Congratulations," he said. "For being Canadian." The crowd roared with laughter.

Denny concluded his words and introduced Michelle, who spoke for a minute. Then it was John's turn, and then it was my turn. Gulp. There was no turning back now, I thought to myself, stepping up to the microphone nervously. I read the speech that Leah had helped write last night for me to say. I began, "I'm thrilled to be here to represent my mother on this historic occasion." The audience clapped loudly, and I took the opportunity to take a deep breath. I had been so nervous, and slowly I started to relax a little bit. I felt the warmth of the applause coming from the crowd and took a deep breath before continuing. "It's hard to believe that it's been almost twenty-four years since the world lost Cass Elliot. Then, as now, rock and roll was suspected of corrupting teenagers and destroying family values. But my mother recognized the positive power of rock and roll and was one of the first to encourage young people to participate in the political process. I'm grateful for this opportunity to reaffirm my mother's ideals at a time when we celebrate her incredible talent and the brilliance of the music of the Mamas and the Papas," I concluded.

The audience clapped loudly when I was finished, and Michelle stepped back up to the podium. Speaking over the audience, she said, "I'd just like to say one more thing that I know: I have personal knowledge that Cass is sitting on top of that big full moon tonight looking down on these proceedings.

Wearing a size six Thierry Mugler dress and thanking you all very much."

Behind the podium, standing next to John and Denny, a video of that night shows me laughing at Michelle's remark, and even doing an uncomfortable little dance. While it may have seemed as if I was dancing in happiness, it was more like a dance of uncomfortability. Again with the weight innuendos. They never died, even though she had.

After the ceremony was over, we were escorted backstage to the press area. I stood as far as I could away from the other three, trying to allow them to be photographed together. Besides, the boots were killing me by now, as some of the photographs captured. A few of the frames shot that day have me making some pretty funny faces that I know from my expression were pure agony.

The next morning, I was listening to the *Howard Stern Show*, as usual. I heard him say something unkind about me and my weight, in reference to "obviously being Cass's daughter." I was instantly incensed and called Carnie immediately from my hotel room in New York to complain to her. Carnie had been a guest on Howard's show many times and was one of the few people who had the private phone line to his studio. She put my call on hold, clicked over to her other line, and dialed the number from her house in LA. When she dialed through, she clicked back onto the call with me to conference the calls together. When Howard came on, and we were all on the air together, he roasted me for being overweight. He started haranguing me over the cause of my mother's death and the ham sandwich story. I argued back with him, as did Carnie. After I offered to send him my mother's official death certificate, the conversation soon ended. Despite the impetus behind the initial phone call, I remain a Howard Stern fan.

CHAPTER 19

IN THE SPRING OF 1998, JACK GOT A PHONE CALL FROM
Mickey Shapiro. After working together on Carnie and
Wendy's Christmas record back in 1993, Mickey had started
working with Jack as his manager. Mickey had a project that
he was working on for a charity record with Quincy Jones
that would benefit the National Committee to Prevent Child
Abuse. The CD would be released on Qwest Records, Quincy's label. Mickey asked Jack if he would be interested in
working on the project as songwriter and producer. Jack had
accepted the task and worked with his friend Steve Kipner
on the project. Along with one other writer, they penned a
song that they called "Love Shouldn't Hurt." The song was
arranged in a similar fashion as "We Are the World" had been,
with singers trading verses throughout. They reached out to
recording artists who were known personally by either Steve,
who brought in his friend Olivia Newton-John, or to Jack,

who called our family friends Stephen and Stephen (Bishop and Stills, respectively). Mickey brought in Bobby Caldwell ("What You Won't Do for Love"). Carnie and Wendy Wilson both participated, as did Ann Wilson of Heart (no relation). I even got to be part of the chorus and sing along with everyone.

It'd been a while since I'd thought about singing. I'd had problems with my voice since the MCA days, having damaged it in the process of recording. I'd developed the dreaded nodules, blisters that form on the vocal cords. I hadn't had pain; I'd just lost the ability to sing. This was devastating, and it felt as if I'd had my joy taken away. I'd always experienced singing as a connection to my mom, which made losing it even harder.

It was a long time before I had the confidence to try again. But now, slowly, my vocal cords were recovering, and I was regaining confidence. Somewhere inside me I still wanted to pursue some sort of career as a singer. I had some good friends named Bob and Claire Parr, who had lived in Los Angeles for a while before Claire was relocated to work for a record label in Nashville. Both Claire and Bob had been wonderfully supportive of me in terms of helping me to realize that I wanted to give music another go, and they encouraged me every chance they got. Since moving to Nashville, Bob, who was a musician and music producer himself, had built his studio there and invited me to come down to record some songs together. I stayed with them at their house, and Bob and I recorded three songs together on that trip. Even though we didn't end up putting the finishing touches on my Nashville demos, it lit my creative fire again. Singing was part of me, and I could deny it no longer.

While I was still in Nashville, my cell phone rang one afternoon. It was Carnie. She'd gotten a phone call from Al Jardine, who was an original Beach Boy. The Beach Boys had splintered off into different bands and were constantly at odds as to exactly who had the rights to call themselves the Beach Boys and who did not. It was a very complicated situation, and the members were divided into various camps, with Mike Love touring as the Beach Boys and Brian Wilson touring as Brian Wilson.

Al Jardine, the voice behind the vocal on their hit "Help Me, Rhonda," was looking to get out on the road as well. He had a great idea to put together a tour that he would head up. He would hire his sons, Matt and Adam, who both sang beautifully, along with Carnie and Wendy. Carnie had brought my name up as a suggestion, because she's my BFF, and he'd agreed to hire me as well. It sounded like a lot of fun, and I was so excited. We'd start rehearsals in October.

In September, the National Committee to Prevent Child Abuse asked all of the singers to come to Washington, DC, and perform the song for then First Lady Hillary Clinton. We were to sing in one of the rooms located in the Dirksen Senate Building atop Capitol Hill, and we were all asked to submit our identification in advance and be screened by the Secret Service. Off we went to Washington, and it wasn't lost on me how close we were to Baltimore, to Alexandria, to where my mom and her family had lived before I was born. I invited Leah to attend the performance that day, which she did gladly, driving from Massachusetts.

Performing for the first lady was an honor that I will never forget. I was to be taking the part of one of the artists who was unable to attend. I was nervous holding my microphone in my hand. Ann Wilson leaned over and quietly bestowed on me a secret tip for live singers on proper microphone placement. "You'll know you're doing it right if you get your lipstick all over the screen," she whispered. A tip from a rock queen like Ann Wilson? I was truly living in a dream. Later, when we'd finished singing for Hillary Clinton, we were all individually introduced, crossed the stage, and shook her hand. Although I'd always shied away from being introduced as Cass Elliot's daughter, it was one of the first times that I was glad to have touted her name in such a ceremonious fashion. I've always been proud to be her daughter and was happy to have been able to represent her that day.

Getting back to Los Angeles after the trip, I was aware of feeling a little out of sorts. Not ill, per se, just weird. I soon found out why: I was pregnant. Jack and I had been married for a few years by then, and I was thirty-two. The timing couldn't have been better.

CHAPTER 20

WE'D BOUGHT OUR FIRST HOME THAT PAST JULY, with proceeds from a song that Jack had co-written with pianist Jim Brickman. I set about turning the guest room into a nursery. I'd been given a picture by rock photographer Jim Marshall of my mother cradling me in her arms at the Monterey Pop Festival. It was a color photograph, my mom wearing huge sunglasses and a white floppy hat, holding infant me. This seemed like a perfect picture to hang in the nursery, so I had it framed in a bleached white wood frame to match the rest of the furniture. This way, part of me would feel like she would be there in the room watching over her grandchild.

We started rehearsing with Al Jardine in October of 1998. He'd booked a few weeks' worth of studio time at Cherokee Studios in Hollywood, the same studio where I'd recorded a portion of the MCA record a few years prior. We sat on chairs on the studio floor, headphones on our ears and singing into microphones to practice our parts and blend. What an amazing experience to sing harmony with a group of talented singers. Every day was fun, as we learned all the songs and got to know one another. We even tackled "Good Vibrations" and the legendary vocal swell in the middle that comes after the long pause. That part must be flawless in its execution, with each singer coming in on a different note. Frightening, I thought. How would I ever know I was doing it right? I called Denny for his advice, as I often did. Most times it was for things that pertained to business issues with the Mamas and the Papas. He was my touchpoint in many regards, and I asked him how in the world would I be able to remember my notes? How would I ever be able to remember what I was supposed to sing, and where?

"Just pretend that *you* are singing the lead, and everyone is backing *you* up," he explained. "It's easy," he continued. Somehow, when he put it to me that way, it made perfect sense. I didn't forget my place or part after that, and singing those songs over and over again never became boring. Those harmony parts are permanently seared into my memory.

Calling the group "Beach Boys Family and Friends," we were booked for shows beginning in the spring of 1999. There were a few stops and starts due to proprietary issues due to some bad vibrations within the official Beach Boys camp. All was resolved in time to get a few shows under our belts before I was too pregnant to travel by May. Before the last show in Oregon, at the sound check that afternoon, there was a large recliner in my spot for me. The message was clear: it really was time to head home. I was definitely ready to get back to LA and nest until the baby came. Being on the road and traveling while pregnant wasn't easy, but I'd adored every second. It didn't occur to me much later that I had sung onstage while I was pregnant, just as my mother had with me.

The tour continued, and before she left for the show in Philadelphia, Carnie called. I'd asked her to be our daughter's godmother, and she'd agreed. She'd be gone just over the weekend, she reminded me. "You better not have that baby until I get back," she threatened. Laughing, I agreed. I wasn't due for another week, so I thought she was being ridiculous.

Our daughter was born that weekend in spite of Carnie's warning. We had decided on her name months before she'd arrived. I'd bought a dozen baby name books and had been scouring them for the best name for weeks while Jack had walked by shaking his head in confusion. I was obsessed with choosing the right name. One night, looking at the cover of my latest baby name book, titled *From Aaron to Zoe*, he commented, "I kind of like Zoe." I liked it too. It went well with the middle name that we'd decided on, which was Ellen, after my mother. Zoe Ellen Kugell was born on June 11, 1999, at Cedars in Los Angeles. Just like I had been.

Denny called me one day and told me of his new project. He and his good friend Paul Ledoux had written a play about his life, in monologue format. He told me that he wanted to pay a proper tribute to my mom. His plan was to first mount the show in Canada, where he'd been living, and then hopefully bring it to the US in the future.

At the end of February 2001, John Phillips became ill and was transferred from the hospital near his home in Palm Springs to UCLA Hospital in Los Angeles. He passed away a few weeks later, on March 18. It was planned that there would be a musical tribute to take place as a public memorial at the nightclub known as the Roxy on Sunset Boulevard. The Roxy was owned by the producer of the Mamas and the Papas, the "Fifth Mama," Lou Adler, and he was happy to have John's memorial there. It seemed right.

In the wee hours of March 10, 2002, Jack and I welcomed our son Noah Martin Kugell. We had given Zoe the middle name of her maternal grandmother at birth, for my mom. We did the same with our son, after Jack's father, Marty. Our family felt complete.

Denny brought his play to New York in the spring of 2003 and opened at the Village Gate Theater on Bleecker Street: the very street that he'd met my mother on, all those years ago, hearing her singing through the walls of the Bitter End. I flew to New York for the opening night. The show's production company arranged for accommodations, putting everyone up at a boutique-style hotel that felt more like an apartment building. Denny was staying just upstairs from me, and we were able to spend a lot of his down time together. On opening night, I sat in the front row watching Denny as he told his story. He was a born storyteller, and he was in his element. I sat spellbound for the entire show. There were a lot of people there, and it was well received.

After the show was over, we were all back at Denny's talking and smoking the evil weed. I came to the conclusion that I needed to see the show again. Incognito. I wanted to be able to fully experience it without being concerned about anyone else seeing me.

I need to clarify that statement: I had felt very conspicuous the previous night. There had been press and photographers, and I hadn't felt comfortable letting my guard down for one instant. I realized that I wanted to sit alone and watch the show. I did exactly that the next night, wearing no makeup, in the back row. I watched, listened, and wept.

Denny did the show in New York for six months and returned home to Canada in 2004. He paid a visit to his doctor there for a checkup, and the doctor was reportedly floored when test results were received. Denny needed surgery, and immediately. He had an aneurysm near his heart, and the doctor was surprised Denny had been onstage performing with it for all of this time. He would need to slow down afterward as well. Surgery was done, and Denny recovered at home in Mississauga,

Ontario, with his kids, John and Emberly, who were now young adults. Sadly, his sweet wife, Jeanette, had passed away in 1998, and it had been the three of them ever since. Settling into a more relaxed lifestyle in the coming months, Denny focused his attention on retooling his one-man show into a show that could be done with four actors playing the parts of the Mamas and the Papas.

I made sure to stay in touch with Denny on a regular basis, as I always had. There was a day when he and I were on the phone at the beginning of 2007 that I will never forget. He told me that he had been to see the doctor, and that it had been discovered that he needed to have additional surgery for that pesky aneurysm. He sounded different. He sounded scared. I could tell that he needed reassurance, just as I had needed reassurance from him so many times in my life. I had counted on it. He'd always been there for me when I'd needed him, and now it was my turn. I told him that no matter what, I was always going to look out after Emberly and John as if they were my own blood. That I would always be there to guide them, and that I planned to live a very long life. They'd never be rid of me, I told him. And I told him that I loved him.

The surgery was done, and he returned home to Emberly and John. We spoke very briefly. He was very tired but happy to be home. He was home just a few days before suffering a heart attack. He passed away on January 19, 2007, in his own bed.

His death hit everyone, including me, very hard. Arrangements were made for his funeral in Canada, and I had no passport. The last passport I'd had was gotten for me when my mom took me to London to make that record when I was five. Fortunately, I was able to drive across the border with my birth certificate and made it up to Denny's house in Mississauga where family and friends were descending. Michelle had flown in from LA with Annie Marshall, who'd dated Denny off and on for the last few years of his life. Leah drove up from Massachusetts to pay tribute to Denny. We all gathered and remembered Denny together. I love to fantasize that in Heaven, or wherever we end up, that Denny and my mom are together giggling like a couple of hyenas.

CHAPTER 21

JACK HAD WORKED ON AN ALBUM IN 2008 FOR WAYNE Brady, with Jamie Jones and Jason Pennock, called *A Long Time Coming*, the title track a reference to the legendary recording by Sam Cooke "A Change Is Gonna Come." They created a track closely resembling the original version, with Wayne delivering a masterfully beautiful vocal performance. And when the Grammy award nominations were announced for that year, Wayne's performance would garner him a nomination for Best Traditional R&B Vocal. To say that we were all thrilled would be an understatement.

The weekend before the Grammy Awards, I received a voicemail from a social worker located at Marin County General Hospital. She was looking for the next of kin for Chuck Day, as he was in the ICU there. When I returned the call, I was told that Chuck was in the hospital and very ill. Thanking the person for the information, I promptly tried to forget what I'd just been told. I wasn't sure I wanted to get involved.

But I couldn't get him out of my mind, no matter how hard I tried. Even though I didn't like him very much, I still felt a strange responsibility. I called a few times and spoke to the nurses on his floor, and one of the times I called, they put the call through to his bedside.

"Hello," he said. "It's Owen," I responded. "Oh, hi, baby," he said, in a sweet tone of voice. He sounded so happy to hear my voice. I didn't know how to feel. Part of me was glad to talk to him, but I still had my reservations. He told me that he was very sick. I'm not sure why, but I told him I would come to see him. Somewhere inside of me, I must have realized that it was important to set things straight. I would head up to San Francisco as soon as I could, I assured him.

But before that, Jack and I dressed to the nines on February 8, 2009, and made our way to the Staples Center in downtown LA. Walking into the show, down the back of the red carpet, we were soon ensconced in one of the many private VIP areas on the "special" level. Our suite had been stocked with food and drink, and before long, we left the suite to begin making the rounds socially, as one does at these types of events.

Heading to the next suite to socialize as the show was going on, Jack and I were walking through the mostly empty concourse level at the stadium. I noticed a tall man walking toward me with two other men closely flanking him on either side. Recognizing him as former Vice President Al Gore, I poked Jack, fangirling. "Jack . . . do you KNOW WHO THAT

IS?" Jack laughed and told me that he did, and suggested I go and say hello. Jack always encouraged me to go up to people and introduce myself as Cass's daughter, in the hopes that the person I was meeting had known my mom. I was always too shy to do it, and this moment in time was no different. No way was I going to do that. We kept walking and went into the next party, which hadn't sprung for the extra charge for a bartender. I poured a pretty stiff vodka and cranberry juice and enjoyed it before we departed for the next stop on our party journey.

Back on the empty concourse, I noticed the same trio of men walking toward us. Having lost any sense of inhibition after my cocktail, now I was breaking free and walking directly up to the former VP, my hand stretched out before me. "Mr. Gore," I began. "My name is Owen Elliot, and my mom was Mama Cass of the Mamas and the Papas" was all I got out before he exclaimed, "Oh, I loved her!" before sweeping me into a hug. "Me, too," was all I could muster. It was such a sweet moment. Jack told me later that the Secret Service with Gore were surprised at my candor. You have to imagine five-foot-four-inch me, walking with purpose directly up to the vice president of the United States, hand outstretched, like he was just another person. The rest of the night was a total blast, even though Wayne didn't bring home the Grammy. It really is true, that whole feeling of being honored just to be nominated. He'll forever be known as a Grammy-nominated singer. Pretty badass, in my mind.

—■—

The next morning, back into the kids-to-school routine, I found myself sitting in traffic as usual. I was telling the kids about my evening before, what we'd done and seen. I told them about meeting former Vice President Al Gore and what a thrill it had been for me. Zoe was nine, and Noah was almost four, and I tried to explain to them just who he was, in Child Context. I said that he had been our vice president, and that he'd run for election in the year 2000. I also informed my Democrats in training about the fact that Al Gore had, in fact, *won* the 2000 presidential election. I further explained to them that, for one reason or another, the people who lived in Florida had a really hard time counting their votes correctly, and now they were saying that he didn't win. I told the kids how funny I found the coincidence that the winner of the election was also the brother of the governor of Florida. I finished the history lesson with the suggestion that maybe the brothers helped each other. Not completely accurate, but I thought it might make for some interesting chats around Circle Time.

I threw a small bag together when I got home from dropping off the kids and told Jack I was going to see Chuck. I got in my car and drove north for six hours to Marin County. It was late in the afternoon, and the drive had been long. I found a decent-looking motel near the hospital and checked in for the night. The place was clean, besides the two flies that buzzed in a circle all night long.

When I woke up early that next morning, I found a nearby Starbucks and waited for it to open before making my way over to Marin General Hospital. Parking and opening the hatchback of the car, I sipped my coffee and tried to figure out my next step. First, I wanted to talk to the hospital's social worker. I didn't have much information about Chuck, or what his condition was, and I needed to know before seeing him what I was walking into.

Sitting down with the social worker, I told her that I was Chuck's daughter. Saying it out loud sounded and felt strange, but it was the truth. She told me that he had severe COPD and that his heart was in terrible shape. He had been hospitalized for a long time and would be moving into a state-run facility before long, due to his uninsured health status. I let the social worker know not to misconstrue my visit as any form of me taking any sort of responsibility for Chuck, financially or otherwise. That wasn't the reason for my visit. She said she understood and escorted me to the cardiac critical care unit, where Chuck's room was. When we arrived, his nurse informed us that he'd just been given a dose of morphine.

I took a deep breath and prepared to go into the room. I had a manila envelope with copies of pictures of my kids inside. His grandchildren, who he would never meet. I wanted to be able to tell my kids one day, if they asked, that he'd seen pictures of them.

As I stepped into the room, he turned and looked at me. He smiled and seemed happy to see me. We talked for a while, and

I showed him the pictures of the kids. It made him happy to see them, and I pointed out the fact that Noah had inherited my nose, which I had inherited from Chuck himself. Smiling even larger, he remarked, "Well, now you'll never be able to forget me." He drifted off to sleep shortly after making that statement, and I snuck out of the room.

Chuck had granted a friend of his power of attorney, and I met with him before going back to LA. We met in Fairfax, where Chuck had lived most of his later life, becoming a celebrity of the hippie haven. He hosted a blues night on Monday nights at "his" club, a place called 19 Broadway. He'd been a regular for decades, and even had a barstool with his name emblazoned upon it. The owners had loved Chuck so much that when the state of California banned smoking in bars and restaurants, they still allowed Chuck to continue to smoke indoors anyhow. Because he was Chuck. Chuck Day died on March 10, 2009, on his nose-sharing grandson's seventh birthday.

CHAPTER 22

LIFE WAS ALL ABOUT MY KIDS IN THOSE DAYS FOR me. From driving to endless playdates and Gymboree classes, being a mom was the dream I knew it would be.

I found myself missing my mom a lot around the time that I became one. I wondered more than once what I had been like when I was a baby. I wondered about questions a daughter might ask her mother, like how soon did I sleep through the night? When I gave Zoe solids, I would have loved to have been able to have asked my mom what I had liked. But I couldn't. I became increasingly aware of the times where I just missed the idea of having my mom. I wished so much that she'd been here to be a part of my kids' lives.

The next few years are honestly a bit of a blur. Between diapers, bottles, and searching for the "right" preschool, the years fade together. When Noah was old enough to start preschool, he went to the same one that Zoe had gone to. I was thrilled to be able to send them to a private Jewish preschool and give them the gift of educating them in a traditional Jewish way, which my mom had begun to give me before she died. I have no doubt that she would have continued to have me continue my education: perhaps I would have had a bat mitzvah just as my mom had. Jack's family was an observant Jewish family; his maternal grandmother was Orthodox and deeply religious. Jack had gone to a Jewish school when he was a little boy in Connecticut, and our decision to educate our children in a similar fashion felt right. I knew my mom would have approved. That was important to me, because in some way it felt like she was part of that decision.

I was lucky to have been able to stay home full time and raise my kids. Jack continued to work in the music business, writing and producing songs. I did all the things that moms do: drive the kids to school, playdates, and doctors' appointments. I reveled in just being a mom and not giving much thought to anything else.

As she grew, Zoe began to resemble my mom more and more. It was obvious to others before I was able to see it myself, but eventually even I couldn't help but notice. She looked more like my mother than I did, which was wonderfully comforting in a way. One afternoon, she was with a friend of hers, and they were helping the friend's mom at her store. The girls were helping a customer when the customer stopped and looked directly at Zoe. "Has anyone ever told you that you look just like Mama Cass?" she asked Zoe. Giggling, Zoe's friend told the customer, "Well, she *should*! She is her granddaughter!" It wasn't the last time Zoe would hear the comparison; it was only the first. There's something beautiful about the resemblance. Genetics are truly a remarkable thing.

My mom had a friend named Sue Cameron, who had a daily column in the *Hollywood Reporter*. I met Sue at a party at some point in the mideighties. They'd been good friends, though I didn't remember her. Sue had met my mom in 1966 when the Mamas and the Papas had their first hit and were performing it on the TV show *Shivaree*. Sue walked up to my mother, introduced herself at rehearsal, and asked to interview the group. After the interview, Sue and my mother discovered they were neighbors, living five blocks away from one another in Laurel Canyon. They would spend afternoons at each other's homes and went to Hollywood parties together. Sue also shared wonderful memories with me of the times that she and my mom had been tennis pals, around the time in the early seventies when my mom had begun to exercise more. She'd taken me with her to practice at the Hollywood Tennis Club, located on the Columbia Pictures lot in a soundstage that would later be the home of *General Hospital*. I'd run around and chase the stray tennis balls as they played. They had even dined together at Mr. Chow in Beverly Hills a few days before my mom left for London. According to Sue, I'd been there too, but I don't recall. Sue also told me that my mom had asked her to come to London to see the show, but Sue had to work and was unable to go.

Sue made sure to keep in touch with me, and we became friends. It was so amazing to be able to speak with someone who'd actually known my mom and been her friend. For me, it had always been about trying to piece together everything that I knew about my mom, because I knew so little about her. I'd only had seven and a half years with her. Every bit of information that I could learn about her added to the picture I was building in my mind.

On a weekday afternoon around 2000, I met Sue for lunch at the Beverly Glen Centre, which was near my kids' school. We sat at a table for two and visited for a while talking about my mom. I told Sue that, after all these years that still I didn't know where that stupid story about the ham sandwich had come from. No sooner did I get the words out of my mouth, than Sue looked at me and sighed. As she rearranged her silverware uncomfortably, she said, "I did it."

"What?" I asked.

"I did it. I wrote the story," she said.

Explaining further, she said that on the morning of July 29, she'd arrived at her office at the *Hollywood Reporter*. The writers were all gathered around the central table when she got there, speaking in hushed tones of voice. Seeing Sue, one of them called out to her, "Hey, Sue! You're friends with Cass Elliot. How does she spell her name? One 't' or two?"

Sue replied, "One. Why?" The writer responded, "Oh, she's dead."

Rushing to her office and closing the door, she picked up her telephone and called Allan Carr, my mom's manager, who was in London. When he answered the phone, he was upset and shocked. He didn't know what to tell the press. There were going to be questions, and there were going to be conclusions drawn. The rock-and-roll lifestyle is legendary, and its habits of ill had already claimed many of her contemporaries. Jimi, Janis, and Jim were all gone. Allan Carr didn't need or want people to speculate, and he had a plan. He'd seen a sandwich by her bedside, so he concocted a story. He just needed Sue to write it, which she had done, to protect her friend until there was more information.

Telling me about it on that day in the restaurant, I'd like to think that Sue felt a degree of relief in her admission to me. I know that I felt as if I'd finally gotten an answer to the eternal question of where the story had come from, who had made it up, and for what reason. Now I knew it had been for the protection of my mother's name and legacy.

Wilson Phillips had reunited by 2003 and had put out a couple of CDs since. They had decided to make a CD in 2012 that would be a tribute to their lineage, composed solely of hits by the Beach Boys and the Mamas and the Papas. Among the songs that they were recording of the Mamas and the Papas was "Dedicated to the One I Love." Wendy was singing the lead soprano part that Michelle Phillips had sung on the original recording, and Carnie asked me if I would sing on it as well, on my mom's signature part in the song: "And it's something that everybody needs . . . ," which I did happily. In some way, we'd all come full circle since the days on Carnie's bedroom floor singing "Dog and Butterfly." We were all grown up now, and we all had husbands and kids and lives. Still, there was music. When the girls toured and the shows came to LA, they'd always ask me to come and sing "Dedicated" with them. Even though my shyness almost always made me inclined to stand off to the side, Carnie always tried to help me feel comfortable and at ease on stage.

In 2013, Jack brought up the idea to me about trying to get a star on the Hollywood Walk of Fame for my mom. Initially, I vetoed the idea because I thought the Walk of Fame along famed Hollywood Boulevard was cheesy. I think, having grown up in LA, Hollywood to us locals was a place that we weren't allowed to be after dark. Always crowded with tourists, and later with homeless and runaway kids, it wasn't safe. Jack hadn't been born in LA, so he had more of a fascination with Hollywood. He convinced me that my mom having a star on the Walk of Fame was imperative to her legacy and memory. We applied to the Hollywood Chamber of Commerce, which owns and controls the Hollywood Walk of Fame. My mom wasn't chosen. I found out later that only one posthumous star is granted per year, and that there were dozens of applications every year. The chamber did keep the application on file, and the next year she was chosen. Now came the fun part: finding the money to pay for it. That was on me.

Uncle Joe got sick in August 2016. When Leah called and told me he was in the hospital, I made arrangements to travel to Massachusetts immediately. The news wasn't good. Uncle Joe was terminally ill with cancer. There wouldn't be much time left. Together as a family we decided the best thing to do was to bring him home to Leah's house and love on him for as long as we had. We did just that. Time was spent with cousins who came to visit with him, sitting on the front porch that fall. I stayed through November, sleeping in my old bedroom at Leah's house. It almost felt as if no time had passed since the last time I had slept there. The pattern of light that crept onto the walls at night from the streetlight outside was exactly the same as it had been all those years before. When the first snowfall occurred, and the snow built up on the power lines, I remembered how I used to be able to judge that there would be a snow day for school. Jack took care of things in Los Angeles; Noah started high school that September. Zoe was going to a new school, too. Although I was homesick for my kids and my husband, I knew that spending time with Uncle Joe was important. He was my only uncle.

Joe was eighteen when "California Dreamin'" was a hit. He'd been a senior in high school with his big sister on the radio.

I asked him what that time was like for him, and he smiled a big Joe grin. "It was pretty cool," he told me. "I got invited to all the parties." Joe, like the rest of the Cohen family, had inherited the proverbial Cohen Honk. He was a very talented singer and an incredible musician. He loved to sing and play the blues and had been something of a lifelong traveler. By the time he was in his early sixties, he'd lived and played music across the country, even becoming a blackjack dealer in Las Vegas at one point to pay his bills. He'd ended up living in Northampton, staying nearby to Leah for the rest of his life. He was my sweet uncle Joe, and he passed away that December, the day after I left to finally come home to California. He is very missed.

I'm going to lift a veil of Hollywood secrets here. Most people don't realize the politics behind the Hollywood Walk of Fame and how it works. The Hollywood Walk of Fame and the Hollywood sign are both juggernaut businesses that are owned by the Hollywood Chamber of Commerce. The stars that have celebrities' names on them up and down Hollywood Boulevard have all been installed for a fee since their inception with the installation of director Stanley Kramer's star in February 1960. The fee, for the most part, is usually tied to a promotional campaign of the moment, a movie release or something of the sort. As such, the fee is normally absorbed into the budget of whatever project is being promoted. The star ceremony is tied to that project, and voilà:

a star on the Walk of Fame. Not in our case, unfortunately. We were able to raise half of the fee in a grassroots effort, asking for donations from the various record labels where my mom had recorded. It took a couple of years to even get that far. Then COVID-19 shut everyone and everything down and bought us a little more time. In the summer of 2021, I was informed that time was up, and unless I paid the $40,000 immediately, my mom's star wouldn't be installed until we went through the entire process again. We'd raised half and, since COVID had hit, we had decided to wait an extra year before sending Noah to college. We could make it work, miraculously, and I wrote the check nervously. There was no turning back now.

We were given a date for the installation of the star: October 4, 2022. I could hardly contain my excitement at the realization that my mom would be part of Hollywood history forever. I just knew she'd be over the moon. The entire family on the East Coast was planning to attend, even some who'd not been on airplanes in decades.

Jack had continued to work as a songwriter and producer and was asked to be part of a group of songwriters forming an alliance to obtain fair compensation from the streaming services like Spotify and Sirius radio. He joined immediately. Jack is a smart man. Not only was he smart enough to marry me, he also could have ended up being an attorney. So, he became part of SONA, Songwriters of North America.

Over the years, streaming services have become the lion's share of all music revenue, including what used to be known as physical sales. Because streaming services were a result of new technology, there were no rules in place as to regulate how much songwriters were to be paid. Because it was essentially akin to the Wild West, everyone at the streaming services made their own rules, and songwriters were getting paid almost nothing, while the streaming services and record labels lined their pockets. It was unfair, and songwriters like Jack were furious. Jack attended many meetings, and at one of them, he met someone who worked with a big banking company and was very interested in donating to my mom's star on the Walk of Fame. I was thrilled.

On a near-perfect October morning in 2022, my mother's friends and family gathered at 7065 Hollywood Boulevard for the unveiling of the star. I'd asked Michelle Phillips to dedicate the star, along with my mom's old friends John Sebastian and Stephen Stills, who hadn't seen one another in I don't know how many decades. Leah flew out from Massachusetts, and Russ and Nathaniel were there too. All of my mom's cousins from the East Coast came out. It was the first time in many years we were all together, and not because of a family tragedy, but for a family celebration of grand achievement. I couldn't help but think of my great-grandmother, Chaya, coming to the US all those years ago all by herself to make a life. That life she'd created had in turn created this moment, this accolade received by her own granddaughter. The American dream.

I started my speech nervously. I tend to talk fast when I'm nervous, so I put notations on my speech to remind myself to stop and breathe. I started speaking, as slowly and purposefully as I could muster.

What a fantastic day. So amazing to see all you people who have come out to celebrate my mother, and her achievements, nearly five decades after she's left us. It speaks volumes of the wonderful human being that she was to be remembered today with such fervor, such love. Of course, she has never really left us, because her voice, and the music that she was a part of creating lives on today, across the world.

I know that wherever it is heard, her voice and the music she created help make life a little brighter to whomever hears it, as it does for me.

This was a grassroots effort from the beginning, and many people helped to make this day possible. So today I want to thank the Hollywood Chamber of Commerce for recognizing my mother and her rightful place in Hollywood history. I'd also like to thank City National Bank, Martha Henderson and Denise Colletta, Universal Music Group, Sony Music, the John Phillips Estate, Jeff Jampol, Kenny Nemes and Max Michaels from JAM Artists, and countless numbers of fans who all have contributed to make this day possible. Her name is forever emblazoned upon this star, and she surely will be remembered for all time.

I know that she'd love this today, and I know she'd be so grateful and blown away by all of you showing up for her. And I know she's here, in spirit. So, this is for you, Mom. Love you.

I'd had to make the choice of how my mom's name would be listed on the star, and it hadn't been the easiest decision for me. When I first considered it, I'd thought that "Cass Elliot" would be the way to go, as my mom had never necessarily liked being called "Mama" Cass. The moniker of "Mama" had always felt like a reference to her size—that is, "Big Mama"—and she hated that. I was faced with a dilemma now, because most people only knew her as Mama Cass. She hadn't lived long enough of a life to have been able to shed the "Mama" image, though she likely would have eventually. But she hadn't been given the gift of a long life, and I knew that it is my responsibility to make sure that her life and legacy are well remembered. I realized that the star should be listed as "Mama" Cass Elliot, with Mama in quotes as the nickname that it was. It just felt like it was the way it should be, and that's the way it reads today.

The ceremony was awesome, and I barely remember the party we threw afterward. I was so happy, so over the moon about the entire day. I was in a bit of a haze, a sort of surreal emotional place. Completely dazzled, and I remained so for days afterward.

—■—

It had been like a dream, and I was still riding that emotional wave a few days later when Jack suggested we go to Hollywood to see the star on a regular day. He had also wanted to bring some of the cookies that we'd had made to the people who owned the building in front of where my mom's star was located. They had allowed us to use the steps on their property for extra standing room on the day of the ceremony. It had been lovely of them to allow us to do that, so we decided to bring the cookies as a small thank-you. When we arrived, the man who had been our contact there came out to greet us, and we stood talking for a few minutes. After a second or two in discussion, I couldn't help but turn to look for another moment at my mom's star. It would be there forever, long after I'm on this planet, with her name literally cemented into Hollywood history. Just looking at it was really cool.

I was standing there, gazing up and down Hollywood Boulevard. So, this is what every day looked like on the boulevard, just a regular day, I thought to myself. Suddenly, along came a woman, looking down at the names on the stars as she walked. She stopped when she got to my mom's star, grabbed her phone out of her bag, and snapped a picture. She continued on her way. It was awesome, and it made everything that we'd done to make this happen worth every second of time and energy. I knew my mom would have felt the same way.

So, this too is for you, Mom. Love you.

EPILOGUE

WRITING THIS BOOK WAS MORE THAN A LABOR OF love for me. It was a necessary part of my evolution as a human being. Weaving together all the stories that I have been told over the years about my mom with my own memories has been cathartic in ways that I never could have imagined. I'm left with the most incredible feeling of completion and gratitude for this experience.

The positivity that my mom embodied was contagious. Her struggle and subsequent success as a big woman in a male-dominated business are awe inspiring. She persevered, never giving up. Ever. Central to her legacy is her sheer will to succeed despite the considerable challenges she faced. That, I think, is one of the qualities that people most identify with and admire about her. I know that I do.

I always find myself wondering what my mother would think. What would she think of today's world? What would she think about the many issues that surround us? I know from what I remember and all that I've learned about her that she would have passionate feelings about the state of our country and the planet itself. I've often thought about the conversation that she had with Dinah Shore on her show, where Dinah had asked my mom why she'd felt it so important to get involved in politics. Mom's reply was that she didn't want to someday apologize to me about the condition of our world. It pains me to think that her worst fears may have been realized. Inequality, racism, antisemitism . . . the list is too long to conceive, but I know she'd be deeply disappointed. I also know that she wouldn't sit idly by; she'd have done something.

Because my mom died when I was so little, I didn't know her well and that's always left an emptiness in my heart. Adding insult to injury were the questions and jokes having to do with her untimely death. People *actually* believed that my mother had died from choking on a ham sandwich. It had become urban legend. I grew to realize that it was my responsibility to make sure the truth was told. When I began to dig into her life, bit by bit, story by story, I learned more and more about my mom. One cool thing I learned was that she knew she wanted to be in show business at the end of high school and made a deal with her parents to try it out for five years. If she had not succeeded by then, she'd come home and go to college. She made the deadline by just a few weeks when "California Dreamin'" became a hit in December 1965.

Some stories I was told were accompanied by an actual memory that I'd have; other times, a story would wrap me up like a warm blanket, signifying its authenticity. Having shaped these stories and memories in one narrative, in their correct chronological order, I do think I now know my mom on a deeper level than before. She was funny, smart, sweet, and the most loyal of friends. She's been gone fifty years, but I feel closer to her now than ever before.

I hope that, in reading about her, you do as well. She was quite a woman.

ACKNOWLEDGMENTS

MANY PEOPLE HELPED MAKE THIS BOOK POSSIBLE. First and foremost, I want to thank my aunt/mom Leah for being my mom when mine died, not to mention everything that you have done over the years in protecting your sister's legacy until I was old enough to step in. You taught me exceedingly well, and I am forever grateful.

I must also thank my uncle/dad Russ Kunkel for stepping up and being my dad because I didn't have one. I'm sorry for flipping you the bird under the kitchen table all those years ago.

Nathaniel, you are my brother/cousin. Don't get it twisted; I'm still older than you. I won the cooking contest too.

I want to acknowledge my sweet husband, Jack Kugell, for more than three decades of love and emotional support. To our two kids, Zoey and Noah, for supporting me in this endeavor. Also my in-laws, Sharon and Glen Doernberg and Fritz and Danielle Kugell. I couldn't have done this without you guys.

ACKNOWLEDGMENTS

To the cousins: Ralfee, Deah, Sheila, and Chippi. Look what I did! Love you Ladies of Levine Greatness.

To the wonderful team of people that I have supporting me, you all are incredible. My literary agent, Jennifer Gates, who took the pages I'd written and put them into a semblance of order and sense. Somehow she convinced me I could write this book, with the help of a fantastic collaborative editor. Although I wasn't quite as sure as she was, I trusted her and it turns out she was right. Thank you, Jennifer.

To my collaborative editor, teacher, and friend, Hope Edelman. This book would never have been as thorough and accurate without your guidance. Thank you for not reporting me for stalking you on social media all those years.

To my very patient editor, Ben Schafer at Hachette Books, thank you for giving me the chance to tell this story. It has been everything that I'd dreamed of, complete with the feeling of accomplishment and pride. To everyone else at Hachette, you all are the bomb.

To everyone at JAM Management for helping me keep watch over my mom's legacy: Jeff Jampol, Kenny Nemes, Max Michaels, and David Brake. Thankful and grateful doesn't seem to cover it all.

To my attorney, Ken Anderson. Your continued guidance and surfing skills are mind-boggling.

To Michelle Phillips, I don't even know where to begin. Your seal of approval of this book means more than I can even express. Thank you for always being there for me.

Many of my mom's friends and colleagues shared stories and memories with me over my lifetime, helping me to learn more about my mom. I am so grateful for the funny stories, and the sad stories, too, each one representing another piece of the puzzle for me. To David Crosby, who told me a tall tale or two; Graham Nash, for always remembering my mom with love and grace; and Stephen Stills, for keeping everyone honest. I'm sure that helping you guys "find each other," in whatever capacity she did, made her extraordinarily happy.

I also want to thank Paul Ledoux, Emberly Doherty, and John Doherty from the bottom of my heart for allowing me to incorporate some of Denny Doherty's monologues from his off-Broadway show in this book. This allowed Denny's voice and humor to be a part of the book in an unexpected way, and I know he'd be jazzed.

To Henry Diltz for so generously allowing me to mine his vast archives of photographs for this project. Not everyone can say that their second birthday–party pictures were taken by a famous rock and roll photographer, but I can. Thank you, Henry. You're a mensch. Gary Strobl, you are too.

To Richard Barton Campbell, I am forever indebted to you for your continuing support and dedication to my mother and her memory. Your knowledge and expertise are unequaled, and your friendship is a true blessing in my life.

I have the best friends in the world. I may be slightly biased, but let's start with the Phillips contingent—in birth order so nobody thinks I'm picking favorites—Jeffrey, Mackenzie,

Chynna, Tamerlane, and Bijou. The Sisters and the Brothers. Thanks also to Billy Baldwin, Chynna's husband, brother by marriage.

To my crazy bestie, Carnie Wilson, her sister, Wendy, and their incredible mother, Marilyn.

Elsie (Elsis) May and Gaia Rhodes, Leon Bing, Bryan and Pepper Garafalo, Sue Cameron, Beverly D'Angelo, Sid Krofft, Mickey Shapiro, Kathy Najimy, Robyn Westbrook, Eileen Cope, Laurie Soriano, Jan Crosby, Candy Finnegan, Donna Santo, Michael Mehas, Ernest Romero, Tanaya Romero, Sequoyah Romero, Alicia Yaffe, Jenny Convery, Shannon Ahern. My Western Mass peeps: Donna Hoener, Shannon Carey Bliven, Anna Pertzoff, Elizabeth Hollan, John Panzer. Last but not least, Daniel Combs and Brian Dahl. You keep me grounded, all of you.

MAY 17 2024

WITHDRAWN

GLENCOE PUBLIC LIBRARY
320 PARK AVENUE
GLENCOE, IL 60022
847-835-5056

DATE DUE

JUN 0 2 2024	
MAY 2 6 2024	
JUN 1 2 2024	
JUN 2 0 2024	
AUG 0 6 2024	
AUG 0 6 2024	
NOV 2 3 2024	

**BEST
SELLER

7 DAY**

PRINTED IN U.S.A.